KRS   1/S

WITHDRAWN

HISTORIC CALIFORNIA

IN

BOOKPLATES

by
Clare Ryan Talbot

Author of
In Quest of the Perfect Bookplate

One Hundred and Fifty-Nine Illustrations

OHIO UNIVERSITY PRESS
ATHENS, OHIO   LONDON

Published 1936 by Graphic Press, Los Angeles.
Reprinted 1983 by Ohio University Press.
Reprint prepared with the assistance
of Laurence J. Ryan.

Printed in the United States of America.

Library of Congress Cataloging in Publication Data

Talbot, Clare Ryan.
   Historic California in bookplates.

   Reprint. Originally published: Los Angeles,
Calif.: Graphic Press, 1936.
   Bibliography: p.
   Includes index.
   1. Book-plates, American—California. 2. Books and
reading—California—History. 3. California—Bibli-
ography. I. Title.
Z994.A6C27   1983   769.5   83-7994
ISBN 0-8214-0737-6

DEDICATED
to
Mary and Margaret who have made it possible for me to inscribe this task to the memory of my father, Thomas Joseph Ryan, who loved California.

INTRODUCTION

THE dawn of civilization in California came with the Franciscan, Junípero Serra, and his followers in 1769, but culture as it is now defined did not make its advent until the coming of the Argonauts in 1849 and the years following.

The missionary *padres* strove to raise the Indian from his low state. They christianized and baptized him; they taught him the useful arts of tanning and leather working, of blacksmithing, of tilling the soil, of making the adobe bricks, and of constructing the rude buildings. It was the *padres* who planted the fig, the vine, the olive, and many other fruits that hang in luscious abundance under the ripening sunlight of California's perennial summer. It was the *padre* who unified society, for where the missions and small pueblos were, in the near distance were also the smiling and prosperous *ranchos*. It was the *padres* who left to their successors, the pioneers, the heritage of hospitality and generosity that has made California beloved by the world.

Of the cultural arts there were few, chiefly music and dancing. The former was limited to the folk songs and dances brought from Spain and Mexico, supplemented by the occasional inspirations of Californian musicians. As these latter were traditional, few of them have survived until the present day. Dancing, always an institution, was as popular and as graceful as it yet is. California was the last great child of Spain's declining grandeur and faded splendor, but in strange contrast to other colonies sixty-five years were permitted to elapse before the first printing press was seen in California. There were no schools, art galleries, libraries, theaters, or literature.

There were *caballeros*, handsome and haughty; *señoras* and *señoritas*, beautiful, gracious, and charming. In their daily domestic life and devotional hours there were the frequent intervals of the *fiesta* and the *fandango*. It was the day of the saddle, the *siesta*, and the *sueño*. If there were no libraries, they were not missed, for there was neither time nor inclination to read. It was a lotus life in a lotus land.

At the commencement of the year 1848, California contained about two thousand people speaking English, twelve thousand speaking Spanish, and numerous petty tribes of Indians. She had a few small towns and settlements; her commerce was insignificant; her boundaries and territories cursorily explored or almost unknown; the base of her population nomadic, ignorant, and unsettled; her occupation, the pastoral life; her choice lands and points of approach, covered by titles which had been completed in such a manner as to be a perpetual bone of strife and litigation to her future population; a newly conquered country; her coast unknown; her harbors unfrequented; her merchants petty shopkeepers; her markets the most distant in the world from supplies; laws few and little understood; no exportable products but a few hides and tallow; and to crown all, a year's distance from the governing power—a power whose experience and policy had been entirely pacific and commercial until within a very brief period; and who had just at this time discharged fifty thousand soldiers, restless of labor and panting for new fields of excitement and conquest. Thus she lay—a country peculiarly and most critically situated to receive the coming storm of events.

The coming of the Argonauts brought many changes. The full glory of the missions had faded a decade earlier, and to the newcomers it was but a shadowy name. The pioneers were individuals of restless and driving activity. Many of them were men of education and refinement, and they brought with them the veneration for institutions and the love of traditions which were speedily communicated to their less fortunate fellows. In a report of the Associated Alumni of the Pacific coast in 1865, there may be found the names of several hundreds of graduates of notable institutions. All of these and their kind contributed largely to the development of music and drama, art and literature.

In her extensive researches for the preparation of her admirable essay, Clare Ryan Talbot has found that the bookplate as such seemingly had no existence in California earlier than the Olds label of 1849. In colonial days a few of the missions utilized the *marca del fuego,* and many examples of books so branded are to be seen in the old missions of California.

Bookplates were not unknown to the more cultured pioneers, but they were not to come into vogue until later. In 1878 Flora Haines Apponyi graphically described more than a hundred Californian libraries, many of which might have been notable anywhere, but less than five of the respective owners possessed bookplates.

In these profound researches, the author has established the fact that the rise of the bookplate in this state began as a cultural feature about 1900. Since then it has expanded greatly, and the author has collected notes upon more than a thousand of these interesting symbols of possession and love of books. These reflect the wonders of Nature, the flora and fauna of California, industrial and commercial history, public libraries and institutions, professions and avocations, personal tastes and pursuits. Many of her descriptions are accompanied by historical, biographical, and critical notes of much excellence.

The gifted author, Clare Ryan Talbot, has been admirably fitted for this work. Her intensive studies made during the past five years entitle her to write with authority.

Idealist and enthusiast, with the logical mind and clear vision of the historian, a vivid imagination gently held in leash, a love of truth and infinite patience, she has the happy attributes which have made possible this colorful and worthy feature now contributed to the strangely variegated tapestry of the history of California.

"A thing of beauty is a joy forever."

Robert Ernest Cowan.

FOREWORD

ALTHOUGH the artist is primarily engrossed with permanence in beauty and its delineation according to his particular medium, it is upon his subconscious mind that the contemporary so insistently intrudes. The art of the ex libris, ever the harbinger of the book, is the *avant courier* of progress. That a survey of the ex libris of California should reveal historical influences seems as definite a thesis as can be assigned to the following pages, for it is difficult to chart definitely a theme to that survey which began so casually. As I reviewed these designs in the present era, it seemed as if the years had disentangled the difficulties and left to our epoch the amenities of civilization for which the pioneers so bravely fought. Those familiar with the heady current of historical narrative will not cavil at this veering of the literary craft toward shores other than ex libris. Rather does the resultant emphasis seem justified in the light of the colorful events presented, especially as a new point of view is submitted to those who enjoy the contemplation of any phase of the Arts of the Book.

To this assemblage belong the devotees of the ex libris who are asked to forsake for a moment the more accustomed ex libris listings that they may consider a fabric woven by an historical shuttle. In my opinion, it is indicative of the flexibility and amazing vitality of this miniature art that such a survey seems to reveal the outstanding characteristics of the commonwealth which is the subject of this volume. Therefore the *San Cárlos* bookplate, which appears as frontispiece to this volume, may be compared to the flagship in that other fleet which figured in the colonization of California, though it sails through happier seas than those of 1769.

As might an apprentice seaman, I consulted a master mariner, him whose name appears on that bookplate, who approved the charts for the voyage, and to whom many an S O S was directed during the years of my cruising. The work is terminated at this juncture that readers may contribute further data in the field of bookplates in California, thus aiding the succeeding volume now in preparation. This is asked sincerely, not merely in the customary spirit of prefatorial humility, for only through such cooperation may the work be completed.

.(x).

This essay is believed to be the first ex libris volume to be concerned with the historical backgrounds of a locality. At the outset it was necessary to devise a method of classification of plates which would admit of ready reference. The groups suggested by the arts, professions, and residential divisions seemed to be the most encompassing, and though I was conscious of the fate of anthologists and editors, the resultant chapter scheme was evolved. Though over one thousand bookplate designs were secured through bulletin, questionnaire, and correspondence, this arbitrary grouping proved workable. The only chapters to be composed from the subject matter of the designs alone were Chapters I and VI. Since in some instances professions and residences were not given or were not verified or have been changed, the owners and artists of Californian bookplates will more readily find themselves in the index. As the text was prepared, for the greater part, through material furnished by owners themselves, the exigencies of handwriting must be considered in case inaccuracies are detected, though whenever possible the material was returned to the owner for verification. The original plan to include a complete check listing of all known bookplates in California, with the owners and artists, was discarded for lack of space; but it is hoped that such a feature may be included in the next volume. Therefore readers are assured in advance that I shall be grateful to receive their detection of errors as well as additional data.

A word as to the definitions employed in my title. As I wished to designate as Californians many individuals who are not native, and many whose outstanding service was out of proportion to their years of residence, I was compelled to adopt the definition of that fine old writer, Ella Sterling Mighels: "A Californian is one who was born or reborn here." As selections were made of the designs to be illustrated, primary consideration was given to historical connotation and the Californian scene, rather than to artistic technique, rarity from a collector's angle, or expense in reproduction. In addition to the formal definition of Egerton Castle given in Chapter II, I was delighted to find the interpretation used by that splendid artist and keen student of the ex libris, Margaret Ely Webb: "The chief end of a bookplate is to please one person and to label his books legibly."

I was especially fortunate in securing the approbation of Robert Ernest Cowan, whose unfailing interest obtained throughout the work, even to his eloquent introductory picture of early California. To Catherine Coffin Phillips I am no less indebted for historical advice, as well as for the

.(x i).

stimulus of her splendid enthusiasms. To Louise E. Winterburn, Edith Emerson Spencer, Katharine French Burnham, and Olive Percival I am grateful for kindnesses innumerable, quite as much as for their steadfast friendship. Their extensive collections and ex libris libraries, as well as those of Mrs. Phillips, were placed at my disposal. Among librarians who have given helpful advice I wish to mention Leslie L. Bliss of the Huntington Library and Eric Ellert of the Reference Department of the same institution; Laura E. Cooley and Gladys E. Caldwell of the Los Angeles Public Library; Bess Yates of the Glendale Public Library; Lenala Martin of the Lassen County Library; Mabel E. Gillis of the Sacramento State Library; Nathan van Patten and Jeannette Hitchcock of the Stanford University Library; Dr. Herbert Eugene Bolton, Professor Herbert Ingram Priestly, and Eleanor Martin of the Bancroft Library of the University of California; and J. C. Rowell, librarian emeritus and archivist of the same institution. To the photostatic departments of the Huntington Library and the University of California I am also grateful for favors.

Through the kindness of His Grace, the Most Reverend Bishop John J. Cantwell of the Diocese of Los Angeles and San Diego, I received many courtesies in ecclesiastical libraries. For researches in the libraries of the Franciscans I am reminded of the interest of Father Felix Pudlowski, O.F.M., and Father Joseph Thompson, O.F.M.

The artists and bookplate collectors mentioned in their respective chapters have rendered aid without which it would have been difficult to advance. I am grateful to that sound historical student and distinguished artist, Carl Oscar Borg, for his early appreciation of the plan of this volume, and for the valued assistance of Franz Geritz and Maxwell Hamilton Noll, who have added the field of the ex libris to their other artistic talents. I am conscious as well of the services rendered by the old book shops of California, among which outstanding aid was given through the ever-willing staff of Dawson's Book Shop of Los Angeles. For various courtesies and the loan of valuable works of reference, I thank Eleanor F. Reed and Geraldine T. Kelly. To the indefatigable labors and painstaking study of the latter in liberally dispensing her well-grounded artistic knowledge is due much of the current ex libris interest in the Southland. The Old Book Shop of the J. W. Robinson Company of Los Angeles, A. C. Vroman's Book Shop of Pasadena, and John Howell of San Francisco are also gratefully remembered.

.(x i i).

To many owners who have lent valuable blocks and dies it is impossible to accord sufficient thanks. Those artists and owners who gave or executed sets of bookplates for tip-in illustrations for the De Luxe and Collectors' editions are already mindful of my appreciation; but the listing of their names would too greatly augment these introductory pages. The illustrations for the following plates were supplied as indicated: the R. W. Kirkham from the collection of Eric Ellert; the Thomas Starr King from a volume in Dawson's Book Shop; the Bret Harte from the collection of Olive Percival; the Modjeska from the collection of Katharine F. Burnham; and the Harry Carr by Donald Carr. Copies of the plates of Clara Montgomery and Margaret Thompson have been provided by Mildred Bryant Brooks for tip-in illustrations in the Collectors' and De Luxe editions. Because of the absence in Australia of Ella Dwyer, who etched these plates, Mrs. Brooks graciously offered to undertake the making of these impressions on her own hand press.

Nor must I forget the owners who contributed their bookplates, and a group of friends, students, and authorities eminent in their fields, among which are Dr. Henry Raup Wagner, Dr. Henry H. Harris, Dr. Max Farrand, Dr. Frederick Webb Hodge, Captain George Allan Hancock, Merle Armitage, William Rhodes Hervey, Thomas Southwick, Robert Hitchman, Albert M. Bender, Charles Francis Saunders, John Henry Nash, Ward Ritchie, Samuel T. Farquhar, Phil Townsend Hanna, Agatha Drew Dollard, Elinor F. Cruse, Rey W. Neville, Louise Ward Watkins, the California Bookplate Society, and the Saunders Studio Press.

And finally I am reminded of the patience and interest shown by my husband, Clinton Talbot, throughout the duration of this task, for he was responsible not only for the photographs which are reproduced in the volume, but also for copies of many plates, otherwise unobtainable, which afforded study facilities. For her very adequate translation from the Sala monograph, as well as for her careful editing of the manuscript, I am glad to accord my most generous thanks to Olive Burchfiel.

Clare Ryan Talbot.

La Ciudad de Nuestra Señora
  la Reina de los Angeles de
    Porciúncula
August 15, 1936

.(x i i i).

NOTE TO COLLECTORS OF BOOKPLATES

The bookplates mentioned or illustrated in this volume have been permitted inclusion herein by owners, descendants, or executors with the graciousness of contributing to an historic treatise. The majority of these plates belong to owners who are not collectors of ex libris; in fact, many have been lent solely with the understanding that the contributors were in no manner to be importuned for exchanges. In a few cases the plates are the only copies possessed or known by private libraries, collectors, or estates. Therefore, readers who are collectors of ex libris are asked to limit their correspondence to those of whose similar interests they are certain, or to those whose names are mentioned in Chapter VIII.

TABLE OF CONTENTS

.(x v).

Chapter I

HISTORIC CALIFORNIA IN BOOKPLATES

"Come," said someone, "let us name the new island California; perhaps someone will find gold here yet, and precious stones."

—Edward Everett Hale. *

T HE Seven Cities of Cíbola, the Gran Quivira, and the Strait of Anián! Surely no other nation than that which gave Don Quixote to the world could have outfitted such expeditions and endured such privations in journeying toward the unknown. Yet it was the search for these fabled goals which brought about the discovery of California; fables, to be sure, in which gold was the magnet, for the second voyage of Columbus reported gold at Santo Domingo.

Instrumental in firing the imagination of the age was the appearance of *Las Sergas del Muy Esforzado Caballero Esplandian, Hijo del Excelente Rey, Amadis de Gaula,* or *The Exploits of Esplandian, Son of the Excellent King, Amadis of Gaul,* which was written by García Ordóñez de Montalvo and published in Seville in 1510. Itself one of those romances the subject of a lampooning Cervantes, *Esplandian* enjoyed an amazing sale, passing through several editions and reminding us that there were best sellers even in the half century after the invention of

* See Appendix for starred references.

.(1).

printing. These facts belong to literary history, but for Californians the book is important as giving the earliest references to California, island of Queen Califia, whose Amazon band used weapons of gold and ruled a territory where pearls and the precious metal were found in abundance.

It is thought that Cortés had a copy of this book with his expedition, but the Amazon Queen and her weapons of gold eluded him, although pearls were found. With the gold and turquoise of Montezuma he was familiar, but he knew little of the Golden Cities of Cíbola. It was reserved for Francisco Vásquez Coronado to undertake their exploration after he had learned of their existence from Fray Marcos de Niza in 1539. Undoubtedly an excellent *padre,* de Niza was a doubtful historian, for the "turquoise-studded doors of the many-storied towns" were never found, although Coronado journeyed as far as the present state of Kansas in search of them as well as of the Gran Quivira.

This is the colorful background for the bookplate of Frederick Webb Hodge, a veritable encyclopaedia of information important to the Southwest and California. This distinguished ethnologist and authority on the American Indian has conceived a bookplate which contains the earliest historical reference to California. The other date, 1680, was the year of the Pueblo Rebellion. Juan de Oñate is remembered as the conqueror of New Mexico. Antonio de Espejo, Castaño de Sosa, Francisco Sánchez de Chamuscado, and Don Diego de Vargas Zapata Lujan Ponce de Leon are the names of the chroniclers and explorers who made up this band of *conquistadores.* Although they here form an artistic balance, their

.(2).

actual histories send a modern observer through source books and calfskin folios of several centuries stored in the libraries of as many nations.

The search for information about these conquerors led me to a volume considered one of the rarest of Ameri-

cana. *The Memorial of Fray Alonso de Benavides* was printed in 1630, a thin volume of a hundred pages. Benavides, *Commissary of the Holy Office That Was of the Provinces and Conversions of New Mexico*—according to the title page—wrote an honest, enthusiastic, careful

.(3).

chronicle forming an indispensable source of material of those times. Translated by Mrs. Edward E. Ayer and annotated by Frederick Webb Hodge and Charles Francis Lummis, it was printed in the now historic magazine, *Land of Sunshine,* and is offered here as a suggestion to those pursuing the elusive in print.

On the bookplate, the object beneath the name of Cabeza de Vaca is a Pueblo cloud symbol, and the falling rain descends upon a Pueblo village of terraced houses, "very sightly," as Benavides observed. The feather ornament and masks below, as well as the gourd rattles, are used in the ceremonies given at certain seasons of the year, in which *kachinas,* or ancestral spirits, are thought to be present. The student will find ample material on these subjects in the publications of the Bureau of American Ethnology of the Smithsonian Institution, and the memoirs of the American Anthropological Association.

The gourd rattle is a subject for a monograph in itself, for this valued vegetal product has been of prime importance to the Indians for various purposes over a vast area of the Americas, as has the maize in its identification with our North American domestic history. The ancient gourd, or *calabasa,* was used as a navigating instrument in the South Seas, from which early navigators approached the shores of California. It has been indispensable as a food, utensil, religious emblem, and musical instrument; as the latter, it is a distinguishing feature of Mexican music to the present day. A far cry from Jonah to a Western continent!

The tuna cactus, such a familiar object of Southwest landscape, has also an elusive history, for it was only in Henry R. Wagner's *Spanish Voyages to the Northwest*

Coast of America that its source could be found. The Spaniards first came across the cactus in Santo Domingo and called it *cardon* from their word for thistle. The name was applied to this cactus of the giant variety, its earliest mention appearing in Oviedo's *Historia* in 1535. One of the lower islands of Baja California, in fact one of the names applied to California herself, was *Isla del Cardon,* because of the great numbers of *cardones* around La Paz.

Dr. Hodge wrote of his plate: "At the lower right is a decorated pottery water jar which I dug up at the ruins of Hawikuh, one of the so-called Cities of Cíbola." Hawikuh, the only one of the cities which de Niza saw, is regarded by Hodge as one of America's rarest archaeological treasure houses. Credit is due Louis Schellbach for his successful incorporation of symbols of such significance which were assembled for him by the eminent owner. The plate won an honorable mention in a bookplate competition in 1934.

The Year 1579

Reversing the usual poetic license, it is by "ex libris" license that the next link in this history is represented, for alas, Gaston Schmoll of Paris has thought of a plate which should belong to a *Californio.* However, it is included here because it found its way into the collection of a Californian, because it so beautifully depicts an important incident, and because its subject was noted for predacious plunder.

It was the discovery by Sir Francis Drake of the site of the present Drake's Bay near San Francisco that reminded Spain of the extreme insecurity of her far-flung dominions.

On June 17, 1579, the *Golden Hind* found the harbor which Drake called New Albion from the soil formation which resembled the coast of Devon. "Ye white bankes and cliffes which lye toward the sea" was the journal

Ex-libris

Gaston Schmott

ISMAËL SMITH

entry made by Nuño da Silva, a Portuguese prisoner of war whom the Master Thief of the Unknown World had retained as historian. Francis Drake, as ruthless and vivid as his brilliant Queen, was out to "singe the beard of the King of Spayne," but Elizabeth quibbled not at his piratical activities ostensibly undertaken for explora-

tion. Knighted upon his return, he was a man after her
own pattern, for:

"Adventurers may sail the seas,
But Queens remain enthroned." *

The *Golden Hind,* held in the hand of the braggadocio
captain, is clearly drawn with pennons flying, tugging at
the rigging. Señor Ismaël Smith has scaled the hemisphere to include the scene of the departure, while a
remarkably intelligent whale spouts warning to the un-
scrupulous navigator. The owner evolved the plate from
one of Señor Smith's drawings submitted as sketch for
the medal of *Instituto de las Españas* of Columbia University.

The Year 1701

A design which approximates the Frederick Webb
Hodge bookplate in suggesting controversial points in
early Californian history is that of Laurence Darby
Ryan, who asked the artist, Maxwell Hamilton Noll, to
evolve a plate illustrating his fondness for the art of the
cartographer. The map from which the design was adapted appears as frontispiece in the first volume of Venegas'
Noticia de la California, and has the title, *Mapa de la
California, su golfo y provincias fronteras en el continente
de Nueva España.*

As Christopher Morley once admitted that he reads
the Oxford Dictionary for keen enjoyment, so does the
owner of this bookplate peruse and collect maps of all
types and localities. In an earlier age he might have been
apprenticed to Gerardus Mercator or to Abraham Ortelius; in the present he asks merely that his collection

.(7).

of maps be as disorderly as he pleases and as undisturbed as possible.

This plate illustrates one of the most fascinating incidents in the life of Francisco Eusebio Kino, and at the same time recalls the discovery of an important fact of

California's geography. Kino was a Jesuit missionary whose exploits and manifold contributions have at length emerged from the mists of historical obscurity; and the reader is invited to investigate the material extant upon this heroic figure who is so prominently identified with the history of the Southwest.

Records tell marvellous tales of the organizing genius of the man who was explorer, cosmographer, rancher, and statesman, as well as mighty spiritual captain, the contemporary of Marquette and La Salle. Also he introduced the cattle industry into the Pimería Alta section, thus beginning the industry which became one of modern California's greatest resources. He it was who discovered that California might be reached overland from Northern Mexico. After crossing the Colorado

.(8).

River on a raft and journeying southward, he made the discovery on November 21, 1701, that the Gulf of California did not extend above thirty-two degrees of latitude and that *California no es isla.*

The incident of the blue shells is charming in its simplicity, for these simple objects provided the clue which convinced the explorer priest that the shells had been carried inland and overland from the Pacific, upon whose Western shore he himself had seen similar shells years before. In a letter to Kino, Father Kappus wrote:

"I value the blue shells more than my eyes, especially the large one which is indeed a rare specimen. . . . The other day the Father Rector Juan María Salvatierra sent me four shells from the *contracosta,* and they are of exactly the same sort."

The Year 1769

The march of our ex libris narrative is speeded by the happy thought of Robert Ernest Cowan, who chose the *San Carlos,* the *Mayflower* of the Pacific, for his bookplate. It is as symbolic of the state as of its patrician owner, Californian *extraordinaire,* historian, and author of the famous *Bibliography.* It has been said that scarcely any book on this state may be planned or completed without referring, at least once during its progress, to Robert E. Cowan's well-known bibliography.

Etched in tones of ivory and palest sepia by the artist, Laurance Scammon, the bookplate is a faithful representation of the packet *San Cárlos,* which figured in the sea expedition for the colonization of California at San Diego in 1769. The exact story may be read as written by those qualified to tell it, for Father Serra wrote to José de Gálvez, *visitador general,* a letter which may be found in Francisco Palóu's *Vida,* to shorten the title of the book. When one considers the monosyllabic and single-word titles which have been the fashion for several years, it is interesting to quote the title in full for comparison: *Relación Historica de la Vida y Apostólicas Tareas del Venerable Padre Fray Junípero Serra, y de las Misiones Que Fundó en la California Septentrional, y Nuevos Establecimientos de Monterey.*

Quoting from Serra's letter: "The packet *San Carlos* is a famous sailor, your Reverence may now compare this fact, which everybody saw with surprise with the infamous lies told about the packet, which is without exaggeration one of the best barks that the King has in all his fleets. Indeed, they say that she deserves to be enchased in gold." Whatever were the aspersions cast upon her nautical honor, we are delighted with the fact that artistically she sails serenely on the harbor of San Diego de Alcalá.

The Founding of the Missions, 1769

As the year 1934 was the one hundred fiftieth anniversary of the death of the man whose name is inseparable from any discussion of California, it is well to pause and consider the events which led to the founding of these outposts of civilization bearing testimony today to the zeal and organizing force of Spain's well-founded scheme.

Alarmed by the Russian advance southward from their fur settlements in Alaska, Carlos III in 1769 sent an expedition from Mexico City to effect the spiritual and military colonization of Alta California. Spain's two-hundred-year reign of procrastination, which had not been roused even by Drake's depredations and the defeat of the Armada in 1588, thus ended. Spanish extension programs were always twofold in character: the Cross and the Crown, an invincible combination.

José de Gálvez was sent to Mexico as *visitador general* to organize the government and complete the expulsion of the Jesuits, at that time ordered throughout the world. Gaspar de Portolá was his choice as military leader, and Junípero Serra completed the trio of executive, missionary, and military *intrépidos*. The Franciscans at the Missionary College of San Fernando, Mexico City, were given charge of the missions in Baja California, while the spiritual colonization of Alta California was placed in charge of Junípero Serra, *el padre presidente,* from 1767 until 1784, when he died at Misión Carmelo at the age of seventy.

Of this man it is difficult to write in measured phrases, for he was, as Herbert E. Bolton describes him, "a man remarkable among all pioneers of American history." Born Miguel José Serra on the island of Mallorca, he retained this name until he entered the Franciscan Order at Palma. There he took the name Junípero from Brother Juniper, the favorite companion of St. Francis. This merry lay-brother was greatly beloved of the founder of the Order of Friars Minor, who once remarked: "Would that I had a whole forest of such junipers." A brilliant student, Serra received the distinguished degree of Doctor of Theology before becoming Duns Scotus Professor at Lullian University, which chair he occupied until the time of his departure for New Spain.

For those not animated by missionary zeal, it may be

hard to imagine this brilliant theologian and apologist laboring for the heavenly salvation of a race of Indians which was the lowest order of aborigines ever found in America. But as has been remarked, "religious zeal has succeeded where the cool political judgment of Spain has faded from the picture," and Serra's name is revered in these post-anniversary years, as certainly he never would have sought. His plea for missionary duty was many times refused, but at the very time when the plans of Spain were newly forming, his prayers were answered. He, Father Francisco Palóu, and Father Juan Crespí, "three musketeers of the faith," set sail for Vera Cruz. An eighteenth-century Francis, he emulated the founder by long walks which covered incredible distances. It comes as a surprise to note that at the threshold of his life's work he was already fifty-five years of age.

The story of the founding of the missions is a familiar one to those of us in California. Those in other lands may read of it as told by the ecclesiastical historians, Palóu and Engelhardt, or by the score of eminent authorities from Bancroft to Hunt and Bolton. From 1769 to 1823, twenty-one missions were founded, a day's journey apart, established to form a protection connecting presidio and pueblo, *asistencia* and *visita,* in an ideal communal system.

Considering their accomplishments in these latter days of our much-vaunted plans for specialization and vocational guidance, how was it possible that Old World scholars, of gentle birth, bred in college and monastery, accustomed to the delights of philosophical discourse, could teach trades, agriculture, music, and languages to savages? They were the first cultural agents in this state and gave an architecture to the United States which is

.(1 2).

the only indigenous type to which claim may be laid. The books which they brought from the colleges of Mexico occupy place of honor in this narrative, for the first book-plates to appear in the state of California were contained in those volumes.

The missions were laid out in fertile valleys, each site almost without exception becoming a mart of progress or a future metropolis. The late Charles Francis Lummis observed that the *padres* "never blundered practically or artistically in the selection of sites for their missions . . . and a hundred years of experiment have failed to find anything better than their first judgment." Theirs was a feudal *noblesse* unequalled in North America, the basis of our present-day fortunes, commerce, education, and arts. They have enriched our material progress with a reflection of the more stately culture of the Old World.

Even the highway connecting these missions is our heritage of romance, for *El Camino Real*, the Highway of the King, was established as the official route when California was a part of Spain. It began at San Diego and ended at Sonoma, the last of the mission establishments. Mrs. A. S. C. Forbes, in *California Missions and Landmarks,* gives a detailed account of *caminos reales* in Spain dating from 1236. As we motor over the King's Highway intent upon errands of today, the fortunate few may glimpse, not clearly perhaps, a gray-robed and sandalled figure, walking slowly and remarking: "Even the roses here are as the roses of Castile."

Thus has the bookplate of Chaffey Library been chosen as typical of the mission scene. Borrowed from its proper section of Library plates, it is given here that we may enjoy its detail. Having the quality of a rich tapestry, it

.(1 3).

suggests the tranquillity of scholastic learning, its olive and orange groves prefiguring the industrial wealth to follow. Wilbur Fiske, librarian, explains: "The whole scene is typical of California, and especially does it

embody the rich heritage of natural beauty and productiveness, as well as the evidence of literary culture." The mountain is San Antonio; the *padre,* the old learning; and the magnificent building, the new. The armorial device is the coat of arms of Ontario, Canada, for which the community was named. The plate is the work of Max Wieczcorek and has received an award of merit. Those

.(1 4).

who wish to pursue a thrilling episode in the state's development might read the *Life of George Chaffey,* for this indefatigable pioneer was the developer of the Etiwanda Irrigation Project, the source of the first electric power in California and the precursor of the *white gold* which was later to contribute to the state's industry.

The Year 1775

The *San Carlos* sailed often through the pages of early Californian history; indeed, she must have possessed unusual longevity as well as seaworthiness. *El Toisón de Oro* was her former name. In 1775 Lieutenant Juan Ayala was commissioned to survey the *esteros inmensos* around San Francisco Bay. He set sail from Monterey, and after sundown on August 5 this tiny ship entered the Golden Gate, the first of the Argonauts to come. At this time many islands and points were named, but only three have retained those names to the present day, Angel, Yerba Buena, and Alcatraz Islands.

The late Ray Coyle designed the Golden Gate bookplate for John Henry Nash, whose selection of the harbor of St. Francis is most appropriate. Mr. Nash himself has contributed to the artistic glory of San Francisco as one of the master printers of the United States. "The sunset," wrote Mr. Nash concerning his plate, "represents the rise and glory of art on Western shores, while the presses, printing tools, and books are devices appropriate to my vocation." In passing, it is interesting to note that the name Golden Gate was given to this harbor in 1848 by General John C. Frémont, who conferred this beautiful name after considering the Golden Horn on the Bosporus.

.(1 5).

It has no connection with gold, as is sometimes claimed, except perhaps the gold of the sunset.

Fate, fogs, or miracles! Perhaps it was a combination of all these which hid the harbor from early explorers, for they all sailed past. One incident persists, however, which may solve the mystery. When **Gálvez**, **Portolá**, and Serra were discussing names to be given to the missions yet to be founded, Serra noticed that the founder's name was not among them.

JOHN HENRY NASH

"Don José," he said, "you have named a mission for San Diego de Alcalá, another in honor of San Cárlos de Borromeo at Monterey, and a third for San Buenaventura. But is there to be no mission in honor of St. Francis?"

"If St. Francis desires a mission," said Don José, "let him show us his harbor."

The *visitador general* emerges from the pages of history as a rather naïve individual, for in a letter to the *gobernador,* Pedro Fages, he remarks later: "God seems to reward my only virtue, my faith, for all goes well."

Donner Lake, 1846-1847

The Flavius B. Clement Memorial plate is one in the series used by the Riverside Library. What seems at first glance to be a pleasantly wooded lake is actually the site of the ill-fated Donner party tragedy, whose history is one of the most pitiful disasters in the annals of the state. Charles Woods, librarian, explains it as follows:

"The collection of books which this plate is to adorn is one of about one hundred titles and two hundred volumes, mostly in general literature and art, and for the greater portion, in the French and German languages. The books were given by a highly cultured woman for a long time resident in Europe, as a memorial to her father who was an early Californian pioneer and a surveyor engaged in the construction of the Central Pacific Railway."

In a letter of suggestions to the Edward W. Gentz Studios of Grand Rapids, Michigan, the designers of the plate, Mr. Woods wrote:

"Passengers to California on the Union Pacific, Central Pacific, and Southern Pacific in passing through the Sierra go within sight of Donner Lake. You will, doubtless, find in the Grand Rapids Public Library the work entitled: *The Expedition of the Donner Party and Its Tragic Fate,* by Eliza P. Donner Houghton, McClurg, 1911. Opposite page 71 of the work you will find a picture of Donner Lake sketched about exactly from the line that the railroad follows, the railroad not having been laid out until the late sixties. It is my suggestion that the central portion of the lake be worked up from this picture, the central portion of the foreground clear, with trees set at either side, and a clear view of the lake and mountains beyond. In the immediate foreground to be the railroad with a train and locomotive of the period of the opening of the railroad. Set someplace in the design should be a

.(1 7).

surveyor's transit, and to balance it, a microscope with the use of both which instruments Mr. Clement was familiar." Seldom has an artist such carefully stated details at his disposal, and the result is a happy one. The plate was designed exactly as ordered, except that the

railroad worker's tools and a pioneer gun were added.

The Donner party began its journey in covered wagons at the outset of the overland immigration movement to California. Frémont's explorations, the publicity beginning to center around California, the Oregon expeditions, and other causes led to the onrush of overland travel to

.(1 8).

the new frontier. An account of this movement is given in Cleland's *Pathfinders*. One party of almost a hundred trusting souls started from Sangamon County, Illinois, toward Sutter's Fort as the first stop and supply center after entering the mountain passes of the Sierra.

Through misdirection and an incredible number of accidents, they became lost and were finally snowed in at Donner Summit in October, 1846. When the snows began to melt, relief parties broke through, and on February 27, 1847, thirteen adults and thirty-two children were rescued. It was considered the grimmest tragedy in our history of overland journeys. Cleland named as the "splendid way-farers: Cabrillo, Drake, Vizcaíno, Portolá, Serra, Smith, Walker, Frémont, and Tamsen Donner . . . who walked the paths of hardship to enduring fame."

The Discovery of Gold, 1848

The shot heard around the world of colonial times is parallelled in the Californian flake of gold, news of which "flashed around the world" in 1848. Philip Baldwin Bekeart has immortalized in his bookplate the event of which Hubert Howe Bancroft wrote: "The twelve months of the year 1849 were not so much a year as an age, not so much an episode as an era." And thus was found the gold toward which the Spaniards had travelled in vain. No traffickers in legends were these Dons of the nineteenth century, "for it was reserved for a race sturdier than they, under whose magic touch the golden dreams of earlier days were realized." Or was it that these legends were to be reincarnated in the form of "gold bricks," stocks and bonds? The luck of the forty-niners

.(1 9).

was the luck of the *conquistadores* of sorts, who belonged to a nation which would scoff at *El Dorado,* the Gilded Man, who according to Indian legend dusted himself daily with gold dust as habiliment suggesting his vast resources. Yet it must be admitted that legends pertaining to irrigation projects, railroads, and municipalities upon the sites of somnolent missions became realities only in the hands of *Yanqui* business men.

Mr. Bekeart, who was born at Sutter's Mill (Coloma), writes that there have been six generations of the family in California. Therefore the selection of the subject was admirably fitted to the owner of this plate. The design, engraved on steel by Will Sparks, was taken from Holdridge's painting of Sutter's Mill. The painting was made from a sketch of the old mill drawn by an unknown artist in the spring of 1849. Mr. Sparks restored the painting in 1925 to a canvas nearly seven feet long, now in the possession of Mr. Bekeart. There could be, quite simply, no bookplate more typically Californian, and with the name removed, it might resemble an etching of the world's most famous mill stream

.(2 0).

on the north fork of the American River at Coloma. An entry in the diary of one Henry W. Bigler, Mormon laborer at Sutter's Mill, gives one of the shortest descriptions extant of the event:

"Monday January 24: this day some kind of mettle was found in the tail race that looks like goald, first discovered by James Martial the Boss of the Mill."

The Pony Express, 1860

The story of the Pony Express is another of the momentous events which may be related through ex libris, for the Pacific Philatelic Society chose this most distinctive of Western institutions to grace its bookplate. Very striking in its philatelic tints of violet, orange, and brown, it is a *rara avis* in any ex libris collection. It was impossible to reproduce copies from the original plate, as the die was lost in the San Francisco earthquake and fire of 1906. Aaron Stein designed it. This copy was a gift to the writer's collection from Robert Ernest Cowan, who adds philately to his bibliographical studies. He was secretary of this society from 1897 until 1912.

A discussion of the events leading to the organization of the Pony Express would be part of a leisurely narrative, never more ably related than by Rockwell Hunt and William Ament in *Oxcart to Airplane*. Bill Cody, Joaquín Murieta, F. X. Aubrey, Kit Carson, George Chorpenning—these are names with which to conjure. The need of coast-to-coast transportation began to be felt by America, then in the throes of the Civil War. Although removed from actual fighting, the newly made state of California—for it had been admitted on September 9,

.(2 1).

1850—needed a carrier for its commerce occasioned by the momentous discovery of gold. Finally the first Pony Express was organized, eleven years after the discovery of gold, and left St. Joseph, Missouri, at 7 p. m. on April 3,

1860. The veranda of the old Pattee House was never to witness a more stirring event. But let Mark Twain give the details in *Roughing It,* for there the future irreplaceable American writer outlines vividly the equipment, size of the rider and his mount, speed, rates, and routes with

.(2 2).

the skill of a born newspaperman and the curiosity of a tenderfoot. In truth, it is a kindness to depict this most fleeting phase of our frontier civilization, for it lasted but nineteen months and gave place to the Western Union Telegraph in 1861. Already had begun the Onward March of Empire, with which the history of transportation is always inextricably woven.

As dates are pegs upon which to anchor our thoughts, a few more "firsts" are intruded here. The first local telegraph was established in 1853, a few years before the Western Union. The Pacific Telegraph was operated west of the Rockies, and the Overland Telegraph, east. The union of these subsequently was called the Western Union. Old San Franciscans will recall various humorous incidents connected with the relaying of messages from Point Lobos to Telegraph Hill. The first telephone exchange in San Francisco was established, February 17, 1878, the first in the West and the third in the world. A history of utilities might be a suggestion to future biographers.

The Cable Car, 1873

The fogs for London, the taxi horns for Paris, and the cable car for San Francisco! The plate which is illustrated belongs properly in the section of the University of California, of which Andrew Hallidie was a regent for many years. Although he occupied this position from 1868 until 1901, he is better known for one of the most intricate feats of engineering in the entire history of transportation. It is singular that this administrator to the seventy-times-seven hills of San Francisco will be made known to many Californians through a bookplate.

But who shall have the temerity to question the utility of symbols? More than a typical bit of landscape is represented in this plate, for the present progress and development of San Francisco are due in no small degree to Andrew Hallidie. The cable car was invented to fit the peculiar needs of this city before the days of electricity as applied to street travel. The angle of cable cars out-

UNIVERSITY OF CALIFORNIA
ANDREW SMITH HALLIDIE:
REGENT
1868   1901

lined against the sun, the clearly indicated grade, and the mechanical suspension devices on right and left have been very effectively portrayed by Albertine Randall Wheelan. The wheel and cable at the base are an actual representation of the contribution made to the subject by the Hallidies, father and son, for the matter of ropes and cables had first to be conquered.

.(2 4).

In 1856 Andrew Hallidie made hand machinery for constructing wire ropes, the first wire cable made on the Pacific coast. The suspension bridge as we know it today was one of his inventions, as also were a great many mining devices still in use. In 1871 he developed the idea of moving cars on an endless cable over a steep grade, but the tedious process of patenting had next to be endured. Finally the Clay Street Cable Railroad was set in operation on September 1, 1873, and the indomitable spirit of the pioneer again triumphed over natural hindrances. Clay Street, according to a report of the city commissioners at that time, had a grade of 67 in 412½ feet. Therefore the first cable car operated on a 20 per cent grade. The Mt. Lowe Railway was the result of the combined efforts of Professor Lowe and Andrew Hallidie, who invented the successful device for the 62 per cent grade on Mt. Lowe.

The Great Earthquake and Fire, 1906

This first historic plate of our century is that of James Duval Phelan, revered official, mayor, senator, and benefactor of San Francisco. How fitting that he used the crest from the official seal of the city for his own bookplate, which was adapted and drawn by William Wilke and engraved by Harry French. The phoenix rising from flames is invincible symbol of the courage of a stricken people in a disaster of worldwide fame. It perpetuates the calmness and courage with which the reconstruction of a mighty city was begun. The phoenix as symbol applies not only to the Great Fire, for San Francisco seemed to be marked by Vulcan for his own; from

.(2 5).

1848 until 1851, there were six very disastrous fires and others at intervals through the following years. Those residents of San Francisco who experienced the horror

and the alarm ensuing upon the earthquake shock at 5:13 a. m. on Wednesday, April 18, 1906, must ever read with amusement the naïve description of Portolá, military man of the world, who said of his first earthquake in California, near the present site of Santa Ana, that it was, in a metaphor of his faith, "one half the length of an Ave Maria."

The Olympic Games, 1932

From 776 B. C. to 1932 A. D. is a span of time which staggers the imagination even of those striding through the centuries with ex libris for seven-league boots. Yet the Olympic Games of 1932 are the first to be mentioned in bookplates in twenty-six centuries, so far as we have been able to discover. F. C. Blank was the winner of the Helen Wheeler Bassett prize offered at the contest held by the Bookplate Association International. That the bookplate be given to the winner of the discus throw, John Anderson, was the gracious suggestion of the donor, who noted the fitness of the discobolus design by Mr. Blank. Another bookplate of Olympic Games associations is that designed by Ruth Thomson Saunders for Fräulein Helene Mayer, whose fencing skill is but the prelude to the interests which constitute her a Californian for the present. Athletic contests in the Tenth Olympiad, as in the games of old, were but one phase of the meet; an Olympic Competition and Exhibition of Art in Relation to Sport was also staged by the American Federation of Arts, Washington, D. C. Thus has the fructifying influence of an ancient civilization touched our Western state, over which seven flags have flown in her tempestuous career. An unforgettable pageant of nations and prowess, of dash and brilliance, was enacted in that Olympic year upon a valley not unlike that of the Valley of Elis, for through the golden sunshine and keen dry air of this, our modern Greece, echoes yet linger of *Cérémonie Olympique Protocolaire.*

The Year 1935

In the opinion of Philip Townsend Hanna, one of the most thoughtful students of Californian history, the political aspects of the state's growth have been over-emphasized in considering her important dates or her epochal events. The events relating to the early days of transportation have already been sketched, as well as various influences which have been instrumental in removing so vast an area from a pastoral existence to the status of a modern empire. The succeeding phase in this colorful march might be termed the bridge era, for two of the world's most difficult feats of engineering are becoming a reality in the fourth decade of our century.

The bookplate presented to Yehudi Menuhin by a coterie of San Francisco music lovers contains a sketch of the San Francisco-Oakland bridge at the completion of the first of the spans extending from San Francisco to historic Yerba Buena Island. William Wilke's inspiration has resulted in a plate which thus immortalizes engineering prowess, industrial progress, and the *wunderkind* from whose famed Stradivarius flow chords not unlike the tenuous harmonies of steel spans with their counterpoint of cable and concrete. Through the completion of the bridges across the East Bay and the Golden Gate, the industrial empire of the future will be wrought, and San Francisco, hitherto isolated, will be welded to the Redwood Empire and the northern interior valleys of the state.

. . . . .

Saints and ships and gold! What a different pattern would emerge if history were to be rewritten in terms of recurrent symbols! No wonder that writers on California are accused of overt enthusiasms; it is the groundwork of this romantic trilogy which endangers their measured recital. *Copa de oro,* the cup of gold, lives on in the golden poppies. *Black gold* is the name given to oil, that miracle

.(2 8).

of our modern era, and *white gold* describes electric power. Names of saints live today in mission and city, and lend grace to our everyday language. *El Toisón de Oro,* the Golden Fleece, an order restricted to princes of *sangre azul* of Spain and Austria, was once the name of the faithful *San Carlos.* Spanish gold and the Spanish Main remain to us from our *Treasure Island* days. Are not these the themes which are woven into the gorgeous tapestry of our history from Golden Cíbola onward? Gold in fruit and gold beneath the earth! A nautical litany, explorer ships sail past our shores. The *San Aguedo, San Lázaro,* and *Santo Tomás* of Cortés; the *Santa Vittoria* of Magellan; the *San Salvador* of Cabrillo—these precede the *San Carlos, San Antonio,* and *San José* of Portolá. Would that it were possible to flash upon a screen the bookplates of all Californians; that this cadenced company might be traced through the labels of their books! Surely there never has been a history which reads so pleasantly—a pilgrimage of saints and ships in a frame of gold.

Chapter II

EARLIEST BOOKPLATES IN CALIFORNIA

"The four volumes of Leyes de Indias leave here for you. . . The Curan Filípica has not yet been found."   —Junípero Serra. *

THROUGHOUT this narrative the word *bookplate* has been expanded to connote all its definitions, for the detachable label more usually known as a bookplate is but one of the methods of indicating ownership of books. This fact of ownership is, in my opinion, the crux of the matter, for aside from considerations of how far the bookplate has been evolved from written autograph, crude heraldic device, or elaborate pictorial scene, it is a useless adjunct unless it clearly establishes ownership. In Egerton Castle's *English Bookplates* appears the statement relative to that upon which I base my claims as to the first bookplates in California:

"Now all tokens of ownership in books, whether they be careless signature or seal or stencil-mark; whether they be modest printed name labels, superb heraldic plates, or allegorical compositions signed by some 'little master,' or yet again gorgeous super libros as above described, all these are known in the bibliophile's jargon as ex libris."

While it is obvious that I must refrain from treating of all the clauses in the above definition, though indeed these are all represented in this state within the scope of the subject, it is upon the first characteristic manifestation of book ownership that a new world of bookplates entered my ken. Recording the log of the journey in retrospect, I regret that the process of searching for the first books in California must now be slighted, that the tomes and the treatises consulted must be passed over in silence, and that the moment of discovery of the first books must not be crystallized in its historical import. Traces of books and libraries in the early history of the state are few, those of General Mariano Guadalupe Vallejo, Dr. John Marsh, Captain de la Guerra, and Francisco Pacheco comprising the lot until the early nineteenth century. Bancroft noted this fact, but found that most of the libraries were hopelessly scattered. Therefore it is later than the discovery of gold, in fact, after the influx of the later pioneers had begun, that books or bookplates in the modern sense may be found at all. Thus it was in the very volumes used by the spiritual laborers in the difficult vineyards of the New World that there may be found the first bookplates in these, the first books to be on the soil of California for many years.

Seal or stencil-mark! Now appears one of the most ingenious, legible, and accurate methods of indicating ownership of books that might be found in the entire range of ex libris history. In the books brought from Mexico by the early Franciscans, a *marca de fuego,* or brand, was used to indicate ownership when stamped on the top edge of the leaves or on the vellum or sheepskin binding, a material singularly favorable to the reception of brands and not unlike the hides of cattle.

At the outset, it must be made clear that the subject of

.(3 1).

convent brands is not new, nor were they the product of a frontier civilization. An illuminating volume in this field has been written by Rafael Sala, one of Mexico's distinguished artists, entitled *Marcas de Fuego de las Antiguas Bibliotecas Mexicanas.* The introduction to this volume was contributed by Don Genaro Estrada, Under Secretary of Foreign Affairs, under whose auspices a series of bibliographical monographs, of which the above is the second volume, has been prepared. After glowingly describing Sala's manifold accomplishments, Estrada writes:

"Thus with accustomed patience Señor Sala has reproduced with great exactness and zeal the brand marks which were placed on the sides of books in Mexico during the Imperial Spanish period. How many times have studious men encountered these marks in the chronicles which they were investigating, and how many times have they been unable to identify them! . . All the marks here reproduced are those of the religious orders used at the time, some monastic orders, some educational; and already it is known that in the colonial period the libraries were the almost exclusive treasure of the religious orders."

While the brands of the Franciscan colleges of Zacatecas in Guadalupe, *Colegio de San Fernando de los Misioneros, Convento Grande del México,* and the College of San Francisco interest us most as being the point whence the "three musketeers of the faith," Palóu, Crespí, and Serra, set forth for Alta California, the above volume treats and illustrates brands of all the monastic orders of New Spain. As Sala points out, brands were instituted because of theft in the libraries

.(3 2).

S.ᵘ FERNANDO

S. Fernando

S FERNANDO

Colegio de San Fernando de los Misioneros, del orden
de San Francisco *de Propaganda Fide*, en la ciudad
de México, D. F.

Convento de Santa Bárbara de Puebla, Puebla.

15

.(3 3).

which even papal bulls of excommunication had not deterred. Nor did anathema itself seem to restrain these early library patrons from disregarding or removing the convent stamp and ex libris. These brands began to be used in the seventeenth century. Made of iron or bronze, they were heated red before being applied to the front and back covers of the book, and to the upper and lower edges of the leaves. Often they reproduced the convent seal, thus providing a pictorial stamp easily recognized; again they were a single name, device, or initial.

To describe adequately the pleasure of visits to these old mission libraries where search for *marcas de fuego* led me in my ex libris studies, the mellow pen of a Willa Cather should be employed. A rich reward of antiquarian lore is the prize of the student who would write of these old books, their titles, inscriptions, and annotations so replete with human revelations.

The group of books in the illustration was selected by Father Felix, librarian and secretary to the late Father Zephyrin Engelhardt, official historian of the Franciscan Order in California. Sometimes these books were the gift of secular libraries or of a patron who kindly enriched the mission libraries, for which funds have ever been inadequate. Often marked with brands of other convents, or notes or pencilled data of student or father lector, they contain, on deciphering, quips and questions for the reader tilting with philosophic lance. At random the pages of velvety vellum were opened to reveal that one volume was a book on navigation, not a pious biography. Given by and dedicated to Señor Don Fernando de Valdez y Tamon, Knight of the Order of Santiago, it bore the elaborate quartered armorial bookplate of the navigating Don, in addition to the *marca de fuego* of the College of San Fernando in Mexico City.

In the endeavor to find actual volumes which were selected and used by the *padre presidente,* or which might have come by one of the sea expeditions as equipment for

the first mission, Inventarios of Misión San Diego de Alcalá were consulted, only to reveal that most of those books were lost in an early disastrous fire. But in 1777 a report made by Fathers Figuer and Lasuén of additions to the library listed, along with theological and devotional books, one which possessed special interest: *Medicinal,* by Florilegio. Doubtless this formed much of the knowledge of healing for white man and savage for many years, as

.(3 5).

the unfortunate surgeon general of the *San Carlos* died a few months after his arrival. At Misión Carmelo de San Carlos de Borromeo, one may find volumes which have been inscribed and annotated by Father Serra, as this mission was the seat of his labors until his death in 1784. The letters of the early *padres* are miracles of accuracy but are provokingly noncommittal as to irrelevant data; however, books do enter into their observations, usually in the sense of community property.

The outspread volume in the illustration was sent from the College of Zacatecas in Guadalupe, but the enormous and fancifully executed *Z* is not discernible. This flourish, covering half the page, reminds us of the *rúbrica* without which no self-respecting document might appear, for it was part of the dignity of this race so given to flourishes in manners and customs. The intricately scrolled signature is an old custom in Spain and Mexico, where the peon is not satisfied unless bills and receipts contain such embellishment. Upon the bookplate of Herbert E. Bolton reproduced in the chapter of Authors may be found examples of this curliform art.

These old volumes live as testimony of the civilization which came in 1769, but which is as alive today as the culture of commerce which came with "James Martial" in 1848. Let Crespí and Palóu be consulted for eyewitness descriptions of land and sea expeditions of those arduous early days; and picture for yourself thereafter these very volumes jostling along in cabin and saddlebag on the wearisome journeys by land and sea.

The first known dated bookplate to be made in California is that of William B. Olds, California's bibliographic pioneer, whose library, presented to the city of

San Francisco, became the nucleus of its law library. The Olds plate was made sometime during the last four months of 1849, for William Olds came to San Francisco on August 31 of that year. It is somewhat amusing to note that in the year of that city's most turbulent lawlessness, apparently one of the earliest acts of this lawyer was to busy himself about "contriving his little plate" destined to be the *incunable* of Californian ex libris. Although there are several reproductions of this plate in articles on the early bookplates of California, the illus-

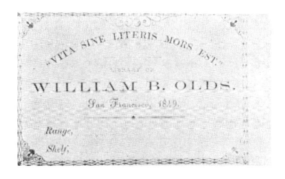

tration is a photograph from one of the actual volumes which belonged to the pioneer bibliophile and which are seldom seen in collections of Californiana. The owner will be described further in the chapter on the plates of the legal profession.

Examples of other early plates will appear in the chapters devoted to the arts, the professions, and the residential groupings indicated by the owners. It is hoped that collector-readers will have further data to offer, for the search has yielded but few to date. Bibliographical value is attached chiefly to plates made in the state and to those which are dated; yet it is hoped that some trace may be found of volumes which might have been brought into the state by pioneers. Quite possibly bookplates could have been brought across the plains by the migratory trains of 1848 or the Argonauts of 1849. Books in a covered wagon would have been luxuries indeed, but what interest would be evoked by a bookplate in a volume shipped around the Horn or slipped into saddlebags on the precarious journey across the Isthmus!

A consummation devoutly to be wished, as well as a suggestion to present-day ex libris artists, which would rapidly advance the science of ex libris bibliography is this: Endeavor to sign and date bookplates. When they may be, and often are, "little masterpieces," why should the credit be deflected to the owner alone? These tiny sketches are remnants of the history of art and society, and the date serves to indicate styles, tastes, and customs in vogue at the time. The single fact of the date has served to establish contested premises in the present volume, and the absence of a date has consigned many plates to an undeserved obscurity. The question of impaired design is a controversial one; yet a simple initial or a monogram or a distinguishing cipher seldom interferes with a composition. And what a boon it is to later historians!

Chapter III

BOOKPLATES OF ARTISTS

"At our departure, our Generall set up a monument: namely a plate nailed upon a fair greate
poste . . . with her Highnesses picture and
arms, a piece of a six pence current English monie
under a plate."   —Sir Francis Drake. *

THE first work of art left upon the land of California refers to the penny portrait of Queen Elizabeth; and the fact that it has prefigured the
dazzling array of artistic contributions of a Western state
seems to constitute its appropriate mention now. *Carte
de visite* left by the elegant freebooter, it is in reality not
a far-fetched harbinger of the bookplate.

The plates of Californian artists possess a uniquely
revelatory quality, for their predominant subjects are
pictorial and symbolic, as contrasted with owners who
use the armorial and landscape varieties. Perhaps a pre-
occupation with abstractions based upon personal am-
bitions and goals is the underlying theme; as if Art, the
exacting mistress who withholds the more she dispenses,
had divinely afflicted those mortals who follow her.

"Rockwell Kent," says one observer. "How like
Merle Armitage," says another, looking at the same plate.
Surely this is a tribute to both artist and owner. Again,
the handwriting completes the design, enclosed within a

.(3 9).

rule scheme reminiscent of early printing. The figure might be humanity striving toward the light of attainment after emerging from the consuming fires of ignorance.

Mention the abstract, and one thinks of angles and set-back architecture, certainly not of charming ladies.

Yet Ruth Thomson Saunders' bookplate for herself accomplishes all this and adds a prophetic touch of literary skill. This plate was designed when the owner was studying in Paris with Fernand Leger, who, when the design was presented for the praise of *monsieur le maître,* added the eye and mouth as a seal of approbation. She writes: "Perhaps I am abstracted beyond recognition; no doubt it is better so!"

"Books revive illusions," is an exquisite blend of sentiment concerned with art and books. Henri de Kruif has used his signature also in autograph, and thereby achieves an individual touch. The owner was the designer of the plate and explained that "in the arts, as in other phases of life, we all chase illusions." The figures silhouetted against the black sky lend a dreamlike quality by their delicate balance.

Marguerite Brunswig betrays a personal talent, for what seems to be a marvellously accommodating bookshelf is in actuality the enormous initials *M* and *B.* Her sculptural activities and interest in modern art have been suggested by James Webb, who engraved the design on steel.

The enigmatic tranquillity of the "unknown woman"

.(4 0).

was drawn by Ralph Mocine for Alice Klauber, the olive leaves a fitting background for the mysterious Renaissance marble.

Reginald Poland regards the mediaeval as the greatest period in Christian art; so it was natural that he used a mediaeval illuminator on his bookplate by Tom Johnson. It contains some peculiarities not noticeable at first, for the monk writes with his left hand. As it happens, this is not a particular misfortune; it merely indicates the tendency of the artist to do unusual things. The grotesques leering from the corners of the monastic

The Property of ALICE KLAUBER and Her Friends

cell represent the gargoyle element in art. The bat is for luck and happiness, and the candle and skull are for the monastic withdrawal which the artist, like the monk, must practice. But among bookplate *curiosae* must be included the bookworm, as lean and hungry as Cassius, feasting upon the folio beneath the desk.

For his art books, Sheldon Chency's plate is an easel holding an unmistakable view of the Golden Gate, though one of the tiniest yet to be noted among the numbers of pictures of this famous body of water. Sometimes the plate is colored by hand to simulate the sunsets, quite truly as gorgeous as the colors he selects.

Haig Patigian's earlier bas-relief possesses the dignity which the sculptural always evokes in the hands of a master. However, the bookplate now used for several years is etched from a pen-and-ink drawing by himself, having the motto: *Plus lis moins sais.*

Margaret Ely Webb has designed several bookplates for herself, the garden plate being well known to artists and collectors, as well as the newer angel-acolyte plate, which is used, as she says, "to mark the owner's approval of quality."

Laura and Sidney Armer have collaborated in their usual media: photography and sketching adaptations. John Adams Comstock has drawn a joint plate for the Comstocks, while the Duncan Gleasons have a ship, as one might have hoped for from the artist of marine and shipping subjects.

Mary Eleanor Curran is believed to be the first ex libris artist in Los Angeles, and her part in the fostering of the art will be related in another chapter. Her flower series is welcome in many collections, the bachelor-button plate being a typical example. The joint plate of Emily,

Mary, and Ralph Fullerton Mocine reminds us of another bookplate artist who has done many plates for Californians.

Not sermons *in* but books *on* stones is suggested by the Indian pictographs on a cave interior, where certain Zuñi signs may be discerned. One of these, as we have already learned, is the Pueblo cloud symbol, for the rain sign of the Hodge plate is used again by Carl Oscar Borg in his own plate.

Another artist, ex librist, lecturer, and designer of bookplates is Leota Woy, who uses a plate which might be the Lady Murasaki herself, in flowing kimono, reread-

ing proof for her enchanting diaries. The letters formed by the overturned bottle of ink betray the owner's name, one which is well known in the bookplate histories of the West.

William M. Conselman, the creator of "Ella Cinders," owns an etched plate by Franz Geritz. The design embodies the Pagliacci theme, which is so fitting for an artist of the comic strip. In it a figure removes a merry mask to reveal his saturnine countenance beneath. Clifford McBride of "Napoleon and Uncle Elby" fame also owns a pictorial plate.

The motto in the border of the bookplate which Donna Davis has designed for herself suggests its symbolism. The charming sketch includes several of the owner's cherished delights: books, gardens, china, silver, and the "clear glow of candles reaching even to the dusty corners." Others who have designed their own plates are Jessie Newcomb Bell Wallace, Maurice Braun, John Adams Comstock, William Wilke, Reginald Vaughan, and Thomas Rutherford Fleming. The Ferdinand Perret Research Library plate, which was designed by the founder and director, suggests that the library is prepared to supply information on all lines of art and the artistic sciences.

Artists from Italy, Belgium, France, Russia, Canada, and America are represented, respectively, by the designs of Leonella Nasi, Victor Stuyvaert and A. Dewinne,

Marguerite Callet-Carcano, J. Rerberg, F. C. Blank, and Margaret Ely Webb. The writer must be absolved from partiality if she singles out for special favor the *carreta* plate designed by Angela S. Crispin for Helen Wheeler Bassett. This is a linoleum cut which includes an example of California's earliest method of transportation in the era typified by the somnolent Mexican and the tuna cactus.

An entire chapter might be devoted to the bookplates

.(4 5).

of the late Helen Wheeler Bassett, for artists' gifts to the founder of the Bookplate Association International represent many of the highest names in ex libris art. She was not a collector of bookplates herself; hence, her personal plates seldom appear in collections. The possession of her plates indicates the grateful acknowledgments of artists, exhibitors, and collaborators in the yearly exhibitions of which she was the director.

The faultless lettering of Maxwell Hamilton Noll is one of two accomplishments of the heraldic artist whose illumination, engrossing, and work in coat armor place him among the notable ex libris artists of the Southland. His own armorial plate for his books on heraldry incorporates the armorial achievements of four families, Maxwell, Hamilton, English, and Kempston, in an excellent example of the type known as the armorial seal.

Since the arrival of the first printers in California, members of that craft have been prominently identified with the progress of the commonwealth. The lively interest in printing today is due to an appreciative audience as well as to the distinguished work in this department of graphic arts. Augustín Vicente Zamorano, secretary to Governor José Figueroa, printed for him the famous—or infamous—*Reglamento Provisional para la Secularización de las Misiones de la Alta California,* the first major piece of printing in the state. It is regrettable that Figueroa and Zamorano did not have bookplates, especially since the country from which they came used the typographical in such numbers.

At any rate, their modern descendants have more than made up for the lack, as there are many typographicals in use at present. There has appeared an excellent account containing a few of the Californian typographicals, written by Edith Emerson Spencer: *Typographical Name Labels and Bookplates of Printers*. Since the subject is vast, the discussion in this chapter is limited to the plates of printers.

Bruce McCallister's plate is an adaptation of the printer's mark of Nicholas Jenson, with which he has combined a reproduction of the famous title page of *Herodotus*, thought by many to be the world's most beautiful type page. This title page was printed by the Brothers Gregory in 1494, but Mr. McCallister has added to it the orange background for  the Jenson device, thus completing a strikingly beautiful plate.

Russell Blanchard wrote illuminatingly and at length regarding the problem of the typographer who would do bookplates, and stressed the fact that "the artist may by a sweep of the hand erase a line, a word, or a letter and put it in again where the effect will be the most pleasing to the eye. Not so with the typographer. He must place his type with the aid of a saw, a file, and small bits of brass and copper the thickness of a piece of paper." The Blanchard plate involved many technical explanations, of which but a few details may be given here. *Date scientiam* is a rendering of the motto of the International

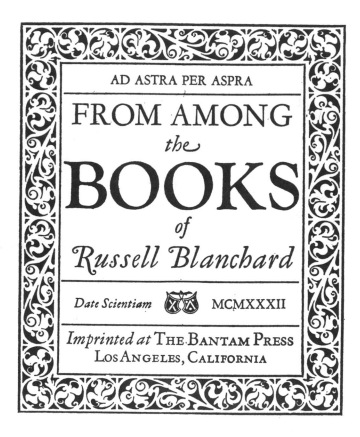

AD ASTRA PER ASPRA

FROM AMONG

the

BOOKS

of

Russell Blanchard

Date Scientiam   MCMXXXII

Imprinted at THE BANTAM PRESS
Los ANGELES, CALIFORNIA

Club of Printing House Craftsmen: *Share your knowledge.* The two shields are the famous device of Fust and Schoeffer, who first used it in the colophon of the *Psalter* printed at Mainz in 1457, the third book to be printed

.(4 8).

from movable type and the first to bear a date. The shield on the right is that of Schoeffer, with a pair of printers' rules forming an angle like that of the Greek letter *lambda;* that on the left is the device of Fust, with the printers' rules *in saltire,* or crossed, forming the Greek letter *chi.* This plate, printed on Japanese hand-made paper, yields a most satisfying effect, combining type, devices, and symbols.

Samuel Thaxter Farquhar's plate combines drawing with type composition, the sketch having been drawn by Lawrence A. Paterson. A god of antiquity has his counterpart in our modern age, for the Winged Mercury, striding over the mountains, spans the continents as easily as does the printed word. The top of Mt. Olympus, from a sixteenth-century map of Ortelius, is used to complete a plate of classic antiquity.

EX LIBRIS

VITA SINE LIBRIS SINE LUCE EST

SAMUEL THAXTER FARQUHAR

Rosalind A. Keep is professor of English and instructor in Journalism at Mills College, and the owner of the Eucalyptus Press. Therefore, it is quite natural that the tree which gives its name to her press should appear on her bookplate designed by Paul Schmidt.

Against a background of the ever satisfying Caslon

flower, H. Wilder Bentley has used the famous line, *Il faut cultiver notre jardin,* from *Candide,* for his bookplate. Ward Ritchie's minute typographical, which is printed in black on rust-colored paper, constitutes the *sine qua non* of the art of the bookplate. Gregg Anderson's plate was designed by Valenti Angelo and printed in red and black at the Grabhorn Press. The typographical of Robert Grabhorn was also printed originally in black and red at his own press.

robert
grabhorn

Chapter IV

BOOKPLATES OF ATTORNEYS

"Lawyers took the leading part in the development of California for the first twenty years of her
life as a state, reluctantly yielding that place in
later days to the man of affairs."
— David Starr Jordan. *

IT will be remembered that a place of honor in this
narrative has been claimed for William B. Olds,
whose bookplate, dated 1849, is the first known
dated plate in California. The gift of the Olds library
to the city of San Francisco made possible its law library;
so the plate has values other than ex libris. The following
notice in the *San Francisco Herald* for March 15, 1859,
gives a few more details regarding this pioneer:

"We regret to announce the death of William B.
Olds, Esq., a member of the bar and formerly clerk of the
superior court and deputy county clerk of this county,
which took place at his residence on Union Street in
this city yesterday morning. Mr. Olds was a pioneer,
having come to this country in 1849, and few men during their sojourn here have gathered around them a more
numerous or devoted circle of friends, or have passed
from its midst more deeply regretted. He was born in
Newark, N. J., in 1824, and graduated with high honors
at Princeton College about 1844. He then adopted the

profession of the law and was called to the New York Bar in 1846. He was a sound lawyer and a polished scholar, and previous to his coming to this country employed much of his leisure time in translating from the French and German for the New York presses.''

Henry Huntley Haight's bookplate is of interest because of the legal and political traditions with which his name is connected. This bookplate is not only the first gubernatorial ex libris in the state, but also the only one belonging to this classification thus far to be noted. The owner of this armorial plate rendered distinguished service to the state, for he was governor of California from 1867 till 1871. His fine private library, described by Flora Haines Apponyi, was especially rich in volumes of Scottish lore and history.

Henry H. Haight.

Hall McAllister, brother of the famous Ward McAllister of New York's ''four hundred,'' also had an armorial plate of unknown date, except that it was before 1900. In a copy of the *Federalist* in an old book shop was found the typographical of Stephen J. Field, one time Justice of the Supreme Court of the United States, and also of California.

Legal and medical libraries have been among the first goals in this ex libris search, since these professions,

.(5 2).

as readers of Shuck and Apponyi will recall, endowed or contributed to many of the private libraries of early and recent times in this state. With a good deal of pride we may point to the fact that although distance and cultural pursuits were difficult in the early days

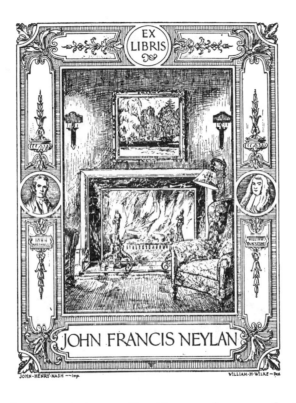

of this pioneer state, collections of several thousand volumes were not infrequent.

John Francis Neylan has employed two vignette portraits of legal gods in his design by William Wilke, which was printed by John Henry Nash. The library interior reproduces above the fireplace a painting, *The*

Black Pool, by Silva, a scene in the famous azalea district of South Carolina. Samuel Moody Haskins' eucalyptus plate is beautifully executed in the woodcut by Franz Geritz.

Still another feature of Californian *silvae* is used by

Edward Dean Lyman, for whose plate Miss McLaughlin has drawn the lacy eucalyptus trees outlined against the waters of Santa Monica Bay. *The assembled souls of all that men held wise* is the motto which completes a design in which the state seals of California and Nevada and the scales of justice are blended with books.

Fine printing and Western history, which are the hobbies of the owner, have thus been incorporated in his bookplate.

Edmund Converse has a plate by Paul Landacre in the design of which the artist has ingeniously indicated

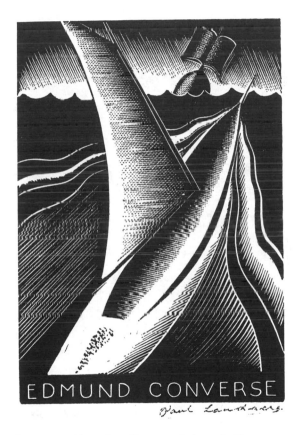

the lawyer's avocation by the yacht and the accommodating buoy which supports an open book.

Of course Charles Albert Storke supplied Margaret Ely Webb with an ideal canting device for his plate.

The scales of justice refer to his profession as lawyer: the pen, the sword, and walnuts indicate his other interests.

The *Pioneer Magazine,* published by Ferdinand C. Ewer in San Francisco in 1854 and 1855, gave Carl I.

Westward the Course of Empire—

EX LIBRIS CALIFORNICIS
CARL I. WHEAT

Wheat an idea for his bookplate. He tells a merry tale of a search for type of the period to use in completing the inscription. He found an old form of Bodoni, as well as a printer's cross-line which had been brought around the Horn. This is the little decorative bracket which appears below the sketch. Incidentally, the *Pioneer Magazine* was the journal in which appeared the celebrated *Shirley Letters from the California Mines,* of which Mr. Wheat edited a recent reprint.

When Judge Charles W. Slack's plate was designed, he was collecting specimens of early Californian gold coinage, including the fifty-dollar gold slugs. A few of these appear in the border of the plate, which was the work of Belle McMurtry Young.

Wilbur Bassett's journeys are not confined to the sea and naval service, as those who know him will attest. His literary and scientific adventures are many, and thus the ship appears as an appropriate symbol on his bookplate designed by Geraldine Wildon Carr.

As familiar a device as the medical *caducei* are the scales of justice in the bookplates of lawyers. Benjamin F. Bledsoe has also used this symbol in his plate, in which the Lincoln book ends bespeak his Lincolniana collection. The heraldic possesses interest for John Farrar Buttrick, whose plate is by A. W. Stott. Lawrence Lyle Larrabee uses an armorial which was designed by James Webb.

Public benefactors, bibliophiles, and civic figures are Alfred and Oscar Sutro, a name which recalls their distinguished relative of an earlier day, Adolph Sutro, with whom the Sutro Baths, the Sutro Museum, and the

Affiliated Colleges are associated. The bookplate of the Sutro Library, which is illustrated and described in the chapter on Libraries, gives a tiny view of the Comstock mine, with which Adolph Sutro was connected. The leather bookplates of Alfred and Oscar Sutro for their personal libraries appear in two sizes and several shades. They were designed by Houghton Sawyer for Bruhn-Elwert and Company.

Sydney Sanner and Joseph McInerney also use leather bookplates, which were designed by James Webb.

Chapter V

BOOKPLATES OF AUTHORS

Scribere qui nescit nullum putat esse laborem. *

IT is a truism that the judgments of contemporaries are myopic and that we are prone to glance backward to the time when there were giants upon the earth. Perhaps that is the reason why I set as one of my goals the bookplates of that royal procession of chroniclers who had been sired by this state from the earliest days of its history. This chapter might have sounded like roll call from the combined rosters of the Bohemian and the Writers Clubs; yet apparently the ex libris traces of Bierce and Norris and Coolbrith are unimportant beside the living legacies of their literary immortality.

Also the section of Authors has been somewhat too thinned through the contribution of their plates to other chapters of this volume. All classifications are flexible, but for some reason literary expression has been the property of many professions. Consequently it was difficult in all cases to apportion talents justly. Writer-doctors, writer-lawyers, and writer-actors have been the history of this task, and in a certain case this hapless editor had to choose from among four established arts and professions before placing the versatile owner satisfactorily.

As nearly as has been discovered, the bookplate of

Bret Harte is the earliest author's plate in the state. Yet as Harte was a graduate of Harvard, it might have  been made in his undergraduate days, though used, of course, in his Californian sojourn.

The bookplate of Robert Louis Stevenson has been difficult to trace, but at last it was found late in this ex libris search, one of the plates which was an early goal. It is a simple typographical, with the owner's name, Robert Louis Stevenson, Skerryvore, outlined by a heavy black line. It was found in a Bible which had belonged to the beloved writer but which is now in a collection of Bibles owned by John Howell. Further interest was lent to this copy, which was printed at the Plantin Press in Antwerp in 1618, because it also contained the autograph of Thomas Stevenson, the father of R. L. S. Volumes from the Stevenson library at Vailima may frequently be found containing the typographical label placed there by Isobel Strong, his step-daughter, for authentication at their sale. Indication that there is another plate might be deduced from statements in the catalogue of the Anderson Gallery concerning this sale in 1914-1916, but at this time of writing, the fact could not be verified. An engraved calling card is often found in other books which belonged to Stevenson.

As unmistakably individual as the hat-and-shoe plate of a later chapter is the bookplate of Jack London, drawn by E. J. Cross. The wolf's head and the crossed snowshoes could belong to no other. A curiously living quality has been imparted to this plate by the sprawling, scribbled haste of the signature, the very

blots seeming a part of this dynamic personality of the Golden Age of Californian letters.

A plate of exquisite symbolism was made by Herman Scheffauer for an owner of the lyre who possessed this instrument by divine right—George Sterling. Since to this gifted writer belonged what Robinson Jeffers calls the metronomic ear, the lyre forms a perfect symbol. Further interest is lent by the humbly characteristic inscription found in one of the volumes presented to the Treasure Room of the University of California by Phoebe Hearst.

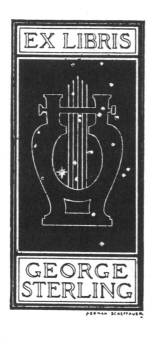

One of the joint writers of *Sixty Years in Southern California* is Maurice H. Newmark, a name revered in the Southland. His plate, Fearing 183, was engraved in 1910 by William Fowler Hopson. It shows a skillful combination of the angling, philatelic, and gardening interests of the owner. Daniel Fearing, in his *Angling Bookplates,* gives a full description of this interesting plate.

Against a damask of laurel leaves signifying victory, Donna Davis has designed for Herbert Eugene Bolton a bookplate which contains symbols of historic importance to the Spanish conquest of America. This is the field of specialization of the distinguished head of the Department of History of the University of California and the director of the Bancroft Library. In this plate the signatures of explorer, *padre, conquistador,* and colonizer are a charming thought, with their rubrics and flourishes. They remind us of this feature of Spanish and Mexican documents which has been mentioned elsewhere in this narrative. Certainly an ingenious protection against forgery, they present unlimited fields

for the experimentation of the original. It is curious
to note that the signature of Eusebio Kino, with its ab-

sence of such ornamentation, seems almost modern in its
type of writing.

The signature of Juan Bautista de Anza ushers mention of his important place in Californian history,
for it was he who made possible the overland route
from Sonora to Monterey and the colonization of San
Francisco. January 8, 1774, was the date of his departure from Tubac, and May 1 the arrival in Monterey.
Athanase de Mézières was called the King of the Red
River Valley. His diaries, together with a sketch of
his life, were published many years ago by the owner
of this plate, and form what has been called the most
romantic story in American history. Don Juan de Oñate

.(6 3).

will be remembered as the founder of New Mexico, and Antonio de Arredondo as the eighteenth-century soldier historian of Spanish Georgia.

Father Kino laid the foundations of the lovely San Xavier del Bac, one of the many missions which he established in Pimería Alta. A delightful sketch of this church appears in the center of the Bolton bookplate. *Luz de Tierra Incógnita,* or *Light of the Unknown World,* was written by Lieutenant Juan Matheo Manje, whose original diaries are being edited by a man who has been decorated by a King of Spain and a King of Italy. Thus symbols of personal significance have been delightfully interwoven into a notable bookplate, not omitting the symbols of the Spanish colonization: the Cross and the Crown, as well as the Zuñi pueblo and the famous gateway of old San Augustine.

Charles Francis Lummis had two pictorial plates; the first made from a photograph of his baby daughter bending over an enormous book; the second, an adaptation of this by Elmer Wachtel, copyright in 1897 and signed by the artist. This bookplate was the vignette heading of "That Which Was Written," the book-review section of the magazine, *Land of Sunshine,* of which Mr. Lummis was editor. His daughter, Mrs. Turbesé L. Fiske, writes: "Whether father immediately began to use it in his books instead of the first plate, I do not know. But I do know that he intended it for his bookplate; however, I find it in use in the magazine in 1895." Possibly further research will clear up the subject, but for the time being it must be taken that 1897 is the date of the bookplate. The earlier plate was found in a copy of *Ramona* now in my possession, a treasured find from the library of the celebrated *Californio*. It was revealed after the Wachtel plate, which had been pasted over it, was removed. The Wachtel plate is shown here.

So enamored was this scholar of all things Californian that he also used a brand, which may be found on fugitive volumes throughout book shops in the Southland. The curious mark at the end of the name is that which may be found on the bookplate of the Southwest Museum in a later chapter. It is the well-known Aztec symbol of the eagle and the serpent, the emblem on the Mexican flag.

Mention of the Lummis name pervades all the chronicles of this section, for few have labored so faithfully to preserve the romance and the beauty of old traditions and inspire Angeleños with the value of their background. "Don Carlos" Lummis died but a short while ago, in November, 1928, and it was then said editorially of him: "He *was* Southern California; he *was* the Great Southwest." He studied Spanish America from Colorado to Chile, and founded the Landmarks Club, to whose activities we owe the preservation of the missions. He also founded the Southwest Museum and was librarian of the Los Angeles Public Library from 1905 until 1911.

The bookplate of the late Sarah Bixby Smith recalls pleasant historic associations, for her *Adobe Days* is a classic among Californians. Incidentally it is one of the few books of early memoirs to contain a child's recollections. A member of the New England Bixby family which settled in California in the fifties, her father Llewellyn and her uncles Jotham and John were large owners in the Ranchos Los Cerritos and Los Alamitos, upon which the present city of Long Beach is located. In a bookplate designed by Maxwell Hamilton Noll, she has used the tree of life, the mystical ash tree of Norse mythology.

Phil Townsend Hanna's tree of life bears fruits which are nouns in the objective case, quite a departure from

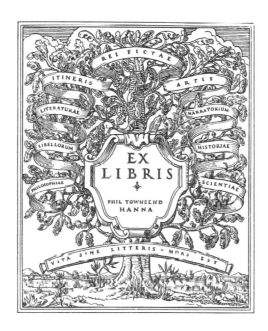

the usual which one has learned to expect from the scholarly editor of *Westways*.

Frank Spearman, whose remote ancestor was a spearman in the bodyguard of Oliver Cromwell, owns a plate in which is a mounted figure forming the canting device. As the plate was designed in 1896 by the architect, Howard Van Doran Shaw, it is one of the earliest of authors' bookplates in Los Angeles.

Henry R. Wagner owns a tiny engraved plate on which *Biblioteca* is suggestive of his writings on the old Spanish documents, voyages, and discoveries. The letters P and R signify *Plains and Rockies,* a phrase used to symbolize his Western books, now the possession of the Huntington Library.

Catherine Coffin Phillips' bookplate is at once biographic, autobiographic, and prophetic, for the tiny scroll on the left explains the use of the home of Jessie Benton Frémont as design subject. The first essay of Mrs. Phillips in Californian history was the life of Senator Cornelius Cole; her second, the enchanting history of San Francisco's storied landmark, Portsmouth Plaza; while the now completed life of Jessie Benton Frémont was under preparation at the time the plate was engraved by James Webb. In this house near her future historian lived the wife of the adventurous General John C. Frémont. From this courageous woman who saw Californian history in the making, Mrs. Phillips first learned many of the tales of the state in whose literary honor she was later to serve.

John Steven McGroarty's genial articles must have been written in the room and at the desk shown in his linoleum-cut bookplate. Rob Wagner's pen and brush illustrate two callings, for he has designed a number of plates for Californians, in addition to editing *Script*.

Olive Thorn Miller's writings on bird life are depicted in her plate by William Edgar Fisher. A study table, comfortably crowded, and a Greek motto bespeak Paul Jordan-Smith's erudite and witty writings. The bookplate of Pauline Garner Curran has one of the delightful flower designs of her sister, Mary Eleanor Curran, the yellow a cheery bit of beauty to glow within book covers.

Entrez, Cappy Ricks, Matt Peasley, Three Godfathers, and the Pride of Palomar! Not a roll call of the best sellers of a decade ago is this list, but a naming of the lovable heroes of Peter B. Kyne immortalized upon his bookplate designed by Frances Troust Daniels, who

has drawn them topping the mast of a windjammer which issues from the leaves of a book.

As one would expect, the bookplate of Stewart Edward

White represents two fishermen floating in a boat near a pine-clad shore. Open books with crossed rods complete the design of the plate in which his signature appears.

Edgar Rice Burroughs, the creator of Tarzan, writes of his bookplate: "It depicts Tarzan holding the planet

Mars, above which are seen the planet's two satellites. Embracing Tarzan's leg is Kala, his foster mother. The crossed quill and saber are emblematic of my interest in literature and the army. The shield in the lower left is supposed to show my interest in equitation, my experience as a cowboy, and my interest in motoring and in books." The plate was designed by Studley Oldham Burroughs, a nephew of the author.

George Watson Cole has one plate of serious nature and one of more lightsome mood. The engraved plate, he says, is "an adaptation of an illustration by Thomas Cecill made in 1630, to which has been added the quotation from the first (1597) edition of Bacon's *Essays*. My reasons for choosing it are apparent, for it represents the three most important phases of my life: reading, writing, and conferences with those who, like myself, are interested in bibliography."

Charles Francis Saunders, botanist and chronicler of the trees and shrubs of California, has a joint bookplate with and designed by the late Elizabeth Hallowell Saunders, in which exquisite lettering simulates an old manuscript.

Lawrence Clarke and Fay Powell have a typographical in which the black hand leaves nothing to the imagination of the borrower. Another typographical is that designed by Ward Ritchie for Leura Dorothy Bevis, the poet whose more mundane activities commit her to the incunabula of old book shops. The first set of these plates was done on Kelmscott paper made by the master, William Morris, and was originally printed in red and black.

Crombie Allen surely must use his plate for his passport, for we know he is an indefatigable traveller. But wait! There's no portrait included. Through the skill of Wallace Bonsall, it states that Mr. Allen came from Pennsylvania to California, from Liberty Bell to mission bells; through clipper ship and airplane, that he is abroad half the time; that he is a newspaperman by profession; that he was ambassador without portfolio during the Olympic Games; and that he is an international officer of Rotary. Passport, calling card, and ex libris, yet it wasn't large enough to symbolize trees, another of the owner's enthusiasms.

Ruth Comfort Mitchell writes that her plate has used a semi-canting device, "for my scriptural namesake was a gleaner." Witter Bynner's plate is an adaptation of one of William Blake's drawings, he knows not what,

.(7 1).

for the volume was lost in a fire in the printing shop where it was made.

In the bookplate of Willard S. Morse, bibliographer of Howard Pyle, a dish of tea is employed to bolster

a thirsty student, perhaps an Oxford don, who pauses a moment from his labors. The plate was designed by Howard Pyle and engraved by W. H. W. Bicknell.

The plate of P. D. Perkins possesses interest from

EX
LIBRIS
WILLARD·S·MORSE

several angles aside from the fact that its owner is the bibliographer of Lafcadio Hearn. An excellent example of the ex libris art, this plate was designed by Takahashi, a Japanese artist famous for his brushwork in executing Oriental characters. It was printed

PERKINS

in Tokyo on starched mulberry paper in tints of blue. The Chinese characters and their meaning are: *yakumo,* eight clouds; and *bunko,* books, or collected works. The waves are symbolic of Hearn's name, which translated is *Koizumi.* From a school in Kyoto where he is professor of English for several years Mr. Perkins writes of his plate: "Thus are symbolized the three elements in Ikebana—Heaven, Man, and Earth. On the left is the name Pe-ru-ki-n-su (Perkins) in *katakana* characters. Blue, as you know, was always Hearn's favorite color,

about which he wrote so delightfully in *Two Years in the French West Indies.*" Professor Perkins also uses seals of his name made in Japanese *hiragana* characters.

Columnists and editors are bookplate owners a-plenty.

The late Samuel Clover had a canting plate which his name ideally represented. Lee Shippey's plate is by Alfred Dewey, who has included all the members of the famous family. Of this plate the owner writes: "The wise mother bird keeps one eye on unwise father bird, so that the little birds won't run out of worms." The late Harry Carr owned two bookplates, the second ingeniously incorporating the first in a design made by Charles H. Owens, an old friend and member of the staff of the well-known newspaper of which the Lancer was one of the best-beloved features. A palm-guarded *ranchito* with red-tiled roof completes the design of the writer who labored as unceasingly as did Don Carlos Lummis for the preservation of the romantic heritage of the state of California.

Chapter VI

BOOKPLATES OF BOTANICAL AND HORTI-
CULTURAL SUBJECTS

"June 2, 1769: Flowers many and beautiful . . .
and today we have met the queen of them all, the
rose of Castile. As I write, I have a branch before
me with three full-blown roses, others in bud, and
six unpetalled."   —Junípero Serra. *

M ANY flags have appeared in the botanical as well
as the military history of California, a fact which
will be noted in a study of the sources, names,
and derivations of our flowers, plants, and trees. These
mute sentinels of the earth have been present as wit-
nesses to the stirring events of the discovery and
colonization of California. The bells of the yucca rang
in unison with the *Te Deum* as mission and pueblo
were founded, and the golden poppies shone no less
brilliantly than the flashing helmets of *soldado* and
comandante. Omnipresent in our travels, subject of our
pilgrimages, arts, and bookplates, they have played
their decorative parts in the colonization of a state,
even as *yerba buena,* the good herb, or mint, gave its
name to the settlement which grew into the metropolis,
San Francisco.

Nature's varied contributions have been easy to dis-
tinguish, for her endowments in Southern climes present

.(7 7).

a startling contrast to those of the Northland where amid the lush moistness of velvety greens are found the dogwood, trillium, and violet. But the paintbrush, which has allowed the holly, spruce, and pine to receive the spotlight, has lavished over the Southland the coppers, scarlets, and purples as if to compensate for the sober tints of cañon and arroyo. Where Nature wastes luxuriantly in flowers, she seems to withhold in the landscape as if accustoming the eyes gradually to such exuberances of color. Therefore, bougainvillaea and geranium are the most frequent accents, in contrast to the gray, silver, and olive-green of the foliage of the characteristic Californian scene.

This interlocking system of Nature's benefactions produces differences in climate and character. Hence it is not strange that, tucked into the corners of Californian bookplates, will be found the poppy or the palm, the cactus or the shrub of the owner's choice. Proof of their ability to constitute a satisfying design is their effectiveness without color, for the ex libris medium is an exacting one. It bears somewhat the same relation to the landscape as do bookplates to oil paintings; as do the old herbals to actual plants. As portrayer of the salient features of the Californian scene, therefore, the ex libris is offered as an herbarium. May this chapter further serve as a reminder to those in less effulgent climes, as well as to those who have conceivably forsaken these mementos *aus einem goldenen Land.*

In the Frederick Tillman plate, Carver 93, a majestic feature of the Californian landscape is exquisitely represented in a design by Henry Joseph Breuer, and engraved by A. N. Macdonald. Seldom in either photo-

.(7 8).

graph or painting has the Sequoia been so clearly depicted. Of this plate the owner writes: "It stands, as it were, for the aspirations of man above all other created living things, steadfast, strong, noble, and upright, its head above the clouds that sometimes shadow our lives." Mr. Tillman is familiar with the little-known fact that there are two species of the tree. The *Sequoia sempervirens,* or redwood, was named by that exacting diarist, Father Juan Crespí. The Portolá expedition, journeying toward Monterey, came upon this species, which abounds in the Coast Range Mountains. Crespí records that on October 10, 1769, he saw "plains and spreading hills covered with high trees of red wood, the trees unknown, whose leaves differ from cedars, although the wood and color resemble them but yet are very different, without having the odor of cedar, and in the trees we encountered, very brittle. In these regions they are very abundant, and because nobody of the expedition knows them, they have been named with the name of their color; that is, *el palo colorado."*

The *Sequoia gigantea,* which has a different formation, grows on the slopes of the Sierra Nevada. Both species are preserved in state and national parks as monuments of the world's oldest living things, whose antiquity antedates the geologic convulsions which formed the Sierra. The writings of Jepson and Saunders may be consulted by those desiring fuller information on the subject. Even the names of this historic species formed at one time an international controversy which ended in 1847 with the suggestion of Stephan Ladislaus Endlicher, an Austrian botanist, that it be named for Sequoyah, a Cherokee Indian who invented an alphabet

.(7 9).

for his tribe. Thus the survivor of countless geologic ages was unnamed until the nineteenth century of our era.

In this chapter devoted to the flora of California, the early typographical plate of *The California Farmer* intrudes its undecorative presence. Although one of the rare early plates in the writer's collection, it received little attention until research was made as to the origin of the naming of the Sequoia. An excellent account of this incident may be found in *Trees and Shrubs of California,* by Charles Francis Saunders, but a few sentences will suffice here.

The giving of botanical names to plants and shrubs is circumscribed by certain rules of etiquette demanded by the disciples of Linnaeus. Briefly, the discoverer of a shrub or plant must describe his find in a letter, preferably written in Latin, and must send the report to a scientific magazine. If the correct *modus operandi* has been followed, the name of the genus stands first, followed by the name of the species, which is usually drawn from the name of the discoverer. On August 8, 1854. Dr. C. E. Winslow wrote a letter to *The California Farmer,* a weekly newspaper published in Sacramento, protesting that the name *Sequoia wellingtonia* was too English for his sentiments. "Why not *Sequoia washingtoniana?*" asked the patriotic Dr. Winslow. Had he but sent this protest to an accredited scientific journal, our

Sequoia gigantea would perhaps have been given the species name of *washingtoniana*. While for botanists these facts are important, for an ex librist one dun-colored typographical has thus narrowly escaped oblivion, and the name of *The California Farmer* is perpetuated.

Certainly the subject of more bookplates than any other Californian flower symbol is the golden poppy, which the Spaniards called *copa de oro,* loveliest flower name in any language. As distinctly associated with our state as is the Stars and Stripes with our nation,

the poppy which carpets our hillsides with blinding richness happens to be the first state flower to have been adopted officially in the United States. This honor is claimed by a slight number of days over New York, whose legislature was then debating a similar topic.

The poppy's début into the botanical world occurred when Adelbert von Chamisso described it in a report to the Botanical Society of Madrid in 1820. Of an exploring expedition sent out by Otto von Kotzebue in 1816, Herr von Chamisso was the botanist, Johann Eschscholtz the surgeon, and Ludvig Choris the recording artist.

An interesting plant found by them in the country near San Francisco Bay was sketched, classified, and sent to the meeting of the society in Madrid.

Perhaps familiar to Cabrillo and Balboa, the poppy has been known by many names since that time, *torosa,*

EX LIBRIS
CHARLES
HARVEY
BENTLEY

amapola, and *dormidera* having been given to it among others, but only *copa de oro* remains to us today. An excellent reproduction of the flower appears on the plate of the California Bookplate Society. Also it is used on the bookplate of Augustin Sylvester Macdonald, where it shares honors with the purple thistles of the owner's ancestral land, interwoven with the motto of the clan.

That the Charles Harvey Bentley plate, Andreini 189, is the only one to be noted thus far which includes the lupine, *Lupinus chamissonis,* is not its sole claim to ex libris interest, for it possesses a majesty comparable to that of a temple "where the Aeaean isle forgets the main." The Winged Victory is outlined against the Pacific marked by the restlessness of the figurehead of the unknown ship etched by J. W. Spenceley in 1906. For this writer at least, it remains not only one of Albertine Randall Wheelan's

.(8 2).

ablest designs, but also one of the loveliest of Californian bookplates, with the classicism of an ancient land happily applied to a youthful one:

"So, gladly, from the songs of modern speech
Men turn, and see the stars, and feel the free
Shrill wind beyond the close of heavy flowers,
And through the music of the languid hours,
They hear like ocean on a Western beach,
The surge and wonder of the Odyssey." *

Although the delphinium is not native to California alone, it should be mentioned on account of its Spanish name, *espuela del caballero,* from its resemblance to a spur. Lovell Swisher raised the garden variety to boast of fifty-seven flowerets on a single stem; hence the leprechaun gardener contemplating his handiwork, as the design for his bookplate. Angela S. Crispin seems to possess horticultural as well as ex libris ability, for her plate contains the botanical variety of gladiolus which has been named for her.

El alisal on the Garner bookplate means a grove of sycamore trees and symbolizes the historic grove near Claremont. The plate was designed for these guiding spirits of the Padua Hills community by Ruth Thomson Saunders.

The blossom of the manzanita is the favorite flower of Louis Edward Hoffman, and appears in the border of his bookplate. *Little apple,* as its name is translated, is the red-barked shrub which grows so plentifully in the Sierra as well as the Coast Range. The plate was designed by Charles Joseph Rider.

In truth, the Spaniards showed real genius in naming the plants and cities of California, and today many

.(8 3).

tributes remain to their poetic discernment. By early explorers the yucca was called *la candela del Señor,* the candle of the Lord. One who has seen this shrub, which advances with pomp and circumstance over the chaparral-laden hillsides from April to June, cannot help feeling with *padre* and *conquistador* that there resides in this plant something to be deified. One of the tallest members of the lily family, it requires from seven to twelve years to reach maturity. Then like the century plant, after years of slow growth it blossoms, sending up a plumy spire of dazzling white. The botanical name for this Paschal candle of the hillside is *Yucca whipplei.* As it gleams in the moonlight on the plate for the Californian books of the writer, it has been fittingly enshrined by James Webb, designer and etcher of the plate.

It is difficult to recognize kinship between the yucca and the grotesque Joshua tree, *Yucca arborescens,* the gargoyle of the desert landscape. It is possible that the first person to see the Mojave desert was a Spaniard. How strange that he bestowed upon this characteristic tree no name from his own tongue, since he had so fittingly chosen the yucca's name. Legend has it that the Joshua tree was so named by the Mormons who believed that the tree was a sentinel pointing the way to their promised land. Of absorbing botanical interest is any phase of the history of this tree. Its survival in the arid desert regions, its area limitation comparable to that of the Torrey pine, and its gorgeous blossoms produced by a curious process of fertilization make a remarkable story in botanical history. Caroline C. Wood has designed her own bookplate in which the Joshua

.(8 4).

CLARE
RYAN
TALBOT

.(8 5).

tree is represented against an effective desert background.

Copies of James B. McNair's plate should be in every camper's kit; though replete with personal symbolism, it shows in exact details the dread poison oak and ivy.

EX LIBRIS

Caroline C. Wood.

With these virulent plants appear the gentler orange blossoms to indicate the owner's other interest, citrus fruit. The distilling apparatus, microscope, and manuscript sheets are the paraphernalia of a chemical and botanical research writer and student.

Phebe Estelle Spalding owns a double-canting bookplate, although the feathery fronds of the eucalyptus, *Eucalyptus globulus,* attract us to a plate whose silvery beauty might be caused by the moon (Phebe), which shines through the trees screened against a sky lit by a single star (Estelle). John Adams Comstock bestowed upon this plate the haze-like glow of fogs emerging from cañon and arroyo; or it may be the light imparted by the heavenly bodies in the canting device. Other examples of this tree are found on the plates of Edward Dean Lyman and Norah McNeill.

Ask any resident of California to name a Californian tree, and he will begin with the eucalyptus, but few know that it is a native of Australia. The name, derived from the tiny cap covering the unripe flower, is from the Greek term meaning *well covered.* By their own admission not always reluctantly volunteered, stamp collectors, ex librists, and world travellers are among the erudite of the land; hence ex librists will not be surprised at the foreign origin of the eucalyptus tree. This fact is well known to those who have enjoyed correspondence exchanges with Australian bookplate collectors, for many of the most delightful plates of the Antipodes use the eucalyptus tree as design feature. In this state it divides the artistic honors only with the graceful pepper tree.

Beyond every land is still the sea.

EX LIBRIS

IRVING E. & ADELE M. OUTCALT

The rarest of all Californian trees, the Torrey pine, *Pinus torreyana,* is preserved in the Irving and Adele Outcalt plate by Annie Pierce. Motorists on their way up and down *El Camino Real* marvel at these grotesque trees, nature-scarred, of which there remain but few on the American continent. They were discovered near Soledad Cañon in 1850 by Dr. J. L. Le Conte, who described them to Dr. C. C. Parry of the Mexican Botanical Survey. Amazed at these hitherto unlisted specimens, Dr. Parry named them for Professor John Torrey, of Columbia University, who had formerly been an instructor of the two colleagues. Until the discovery of the Torrey pines, the record for area limitation was held by the Monterey cypress, *Cupressus macrocarpa.* Today this cypress forms almost as familiar a symbol of the ex libris landscape as does the poppy. The bookplate

.(8 8).

of Christine Price glimpses Monterey Bay through a cypress, as also do the Monterey Library plate by Cornelis Botke and the Julius Wangenheim plate by Alice Klauber.

One might have expected the edible pod or the humble potato on Luther Burbank's bookplate, but Dr. John Adams Comstock has grouped together in his design a veritable bouquet of the wild flower favorites of California: the Shasta daisy, *Chrysanthemum maximum;* the leopard lily, *Lilium pardalinum;* and the beloved rose of Castile, *Rosa californica,* which was probably the earliest flower to be mentioned in the writings of the padres.

The leopard lily is also to be found in the bookplate of Glen Dawson, youthful member of the Sierra Club.

The plate further depicts "a group of Sierra Clubbers taking their noonday tea about a camp-fire in a clearing in front of a large pine, *Pinus ponderosa,* or Western yellow pine."

The cactus in Irma Goldman's plate is the *Carnegia gigantea.* This cactus was named in honor of Andrew Carnegie, through whose munificent gift the Desert Laboratory at Tucson, Arizona, was erected. Another example of this variety of cactus may be seen in the plate of Elizabeth Brainerd Sawe, which is illustrated in the Librarians' chapter. In the linoleum cut of Katherine Wright a banana tree is used as design feature, showing the inverted manner in which the fruit grows.

The essence of spring is found in the *primavera* plate of Edith Emerson Spencer, with its shimmering beauty and exquisite detail. Towering hollyhocks form a background for the slim demoiselle in her mediaeval costume with butterfly coif and graceful tippet, while in the foreground *fleurs de lis* fringe a pool upon which water lilies float. Troubadours might have enshrined this lovely

EDITH·EMERSON·SPENCER

.(9 1).

chatelaine of the garden in their song as she is now enshrined in Margaret Ely Webb's delicate picture. The artist's last perfect inspiration was a border of grass of Parnassus to symbolize the owner's gift of poesy. This plate is sometimes found colored by hand, a treasured acquisition in bookplate collections.

. . . . . .

"Pomona's tent! Here oranges like ruddy lanterns shine;
Cool wine-hued grapes breathe fragrances—Tokay, Port,
      Muscatel;
Voluptuous figs like sybarites in purple silks recline;
The exotic avocado weaves a Caribbean spell;
The olive's royal swartness speaks an ancient Spanish
      line." *

Chapter VII

BOOKPLATES OF CHURCHES AND CHURCHMEN

"Some, being established in peace, strive to establish it among their brethren."
—Thomas à Kempis. *

THE bookplates of the spiritual heroes of the state have occasioned an arduous search, and it is with regret that only a very scanty representation of these mementos of valiant laborers can be made. "It was not what we read of the saints that made them saints; it was what we do not read that enabled them to be what we wonder at while we read," said Frederick William Faber.

A complete history of the subject would include the bookplates of Sunday schools, clubs, organizations, and church libraries; and it is hoped that collectors may bring to our attention the existence of more plates in view of their importance as cultural agents in any locality. Since the mission books and libraries have already been introduced into this narrative, it is but natural to turn to Thomas Starr King, whose statue accompanies that of the revered Junípero Serra in the Hall of Fame in Washington, D. C.

The eloquent preacher of the Unitarian faith, Starr King, arrived in San Francisco in April, 1860, to begin a career of ceaseless activity in behalf of his parishioners, his city, and his state. His oratory and his personal charm were the qualities needed at this stage of Californian history, for he determined the standard to which the state adhered during the Civil War. It is said that he visited every library, public and private, in the city of San Francisco. Thus it was

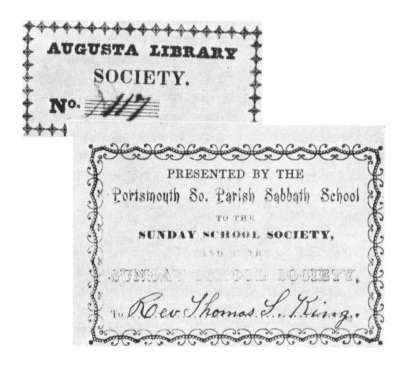

with the genuine joy of an antiquarian that after a fruitless search of many months the name of this inspired preacher was found in a copy of Herman Melville's *Mardi.* Though as welcome as if it were his personal ex libris, it is only a presentation label announcing that the book was a gift of the Portsmouth Street Parish

Sabbath School. A singular coincidence occurred to the writer when she acquired an actual letter of Starr King, the nucleus of a group of Californian items and one of the priceless rewards of this literary pilgrimage. In King's letter written on October 10, 1860, to an unknown friend in Boston, there is an echo of the observation of a Franciscan remembering the roses of his beloved Castile:

"What amazes us here is the roses and flowers that keep blooming in the city, in spite of the sand and drought and chilly nights. A rose bush or fuchsia needs no cultivating. Stick it in the earth, and though the soil becomes packed so hard that you can't dig a knife into it, the bush will pay a dividend, every morning, of lovely buds or glorious earrings. And the way geraniums thicken into hedges and burst into a bloom that imitates precisely the red of an India shawl is a perpetual and delightful mystery."

A bookplate remarkable for its Revolutionary War associations is that of Frederick Turrell Gray, a Unitarian minister of Boston, who used a plate listed by Allen as number 322 and attributed to Joseph Callender. As this engraver died in 1821, when Frederick Gray was seventeen years of age, it is supposed that he inherited the plate. It is another temptation to digress with tales of Madame Turrell, his great-grandmother, who entertained British officers during the Revolution, and whose garden gate boasted as counterweight a cannon ball which was fired by Washington's artillery and rebounded into her yard from Brattle Street.

The residence of the Reverend Mr. Gray in California, though short, was long enough to enter into our

.(9 5).

narrative. Answering a call to the West, he sailed on the steamer *Illinois* for Panama. There he crossed the Isthmus on muleback and boarded the *J. L. Stephens*. He arrived in San Francisco on June 21, 1853, and within four weeks of his arrival he dedicated the society's new church on Stockton near Sacramento Street. His zeal was no less than that of the exploring *padres,* for tes-

timonials tendered during his residence and after his return East are signed with a roster of grateful San Franciscans. The Gray bookplate is included here through the kindness of a descendant, Frederick Jackson, whose plate is described in the Los Angeles chapter.

Plates such as that of the St. John's Church in the Mission Dolores district of San Francisco and other religious plates possess historic value, but their uniformity precludes mention in such a general discussion as this, for they are often typographical and printers' labels.

Ecclesiastical bookplates employ an ancient language of heraldry in which the *armes parlantes* is frequently the subject. Those who know the bookplate of Cardinal Wolsey will remember the cord and tassels which descend from the hat, as well as the knotting of the cord which indicates rank and office when accompanied by crozier and miter in conjunction with the shield.

The armorial leads other classes of bookplates of churchmen, perhaps because it fits so eminently the more serious volumes owned by these men; also because the ecclesiastical arms incorporate the arms of the owner's jurisdiction, or diocese, as well as the arms of the family. One of the plates which the writer values highly is the armorial of the late William Ingraham Kip. A member of a famous old New York family, he came to San Francisco in 1854 as the first Episcopalian bishop and rector of Grace Church. Bishop Johnson of revered name also used an armorial. The plates of the Reverend William A. Brewer will, of course, be mentioned in the Collectors' chapter, as will also the plate of his father, the Reverend Alfred Brewer, rector of St. Paul's Church in Burlingame. St. Paul's Church also owns a bookplate.

The written signature of Francis J. Conaty completes a design of dignity and personal significance encompassed by a devotional symbol of his faith. The musical

.(9 7).

and literary interests of the Monsignor are indicated in the design by Mary Eleanor Curran, who has also shown the exterior and the interior of the Cathedral Chapel of Our Lady of Guadalupe.

Ex Libris

A similar dignity has been achieved by Raymond C. Brooks in a design which resembles a delicate pastel, comprising a view of snow-topped Sierra as seen from a porticoed garden glimpsed through eucalyptus and cedar trees. Developed in tones of silver and jade by Ruth Thomson Saunders, the plate achieves a spirituelle quality of restfulness.

This versatile artist has also designed a plate of Californian associations for the Mary Penfield Norton

Memorial Library of the Community Congregational Church in Claremont. The yucca plate is one which invariably occasions favorable comment in its striking treatment of this majestic shrub.

Monsignor Gleason's *abbé* has a cowl, habit, and merry look bespeaking the mellow scholar. David Ransom Covell, Maxwell Savage, and Edward Morgan are owners of armorial plates engraved by James Webb.

.(9 9).

An interesting fact is preserved in one of the book-plates of the University of California. The plate designed by Albertine Randall Wheelan in 1904 to mark the Semitic books which were presented to the university by members of Temple Emanu-El represents the synagogue which was built on Sutter Street by the oldest

Jewish society in San Francisco. The synagogue was destroyed in the fire of 1906. Trinity Church of Santa Barbara has a plate by Margaret Ely Webb.

William Frederic Bade, of the Pacific School of Religion, has a bookplate in which his coat of arms and the seal of this institution have been used as features by Beulah Mitchell Clute. The redwood branches signify his interest in the Save the Redwoods League. The plate pictures the room in which the owner prepared his distinguished *Life and Letters of John Muir*.

Chapter VIII

BOOKPLATES OF COLLECTORS AND BOOKPLATES SOCIETIES

"The collection of curious things, to those who drive through life toward some definite objective, is a mystery that may not ever be satisfactorily explained, but must always serve to emphasize their own superior common sense."

—Paul Jordan-Smith. *

"ON Saturday, May 4, 1907," says *The Bookplate Booklet* for May, 1907, "seven designers and collectors of bookplates met for an informal lunch at the Paris Tea Garden in San Francisco, with the definite purpose of organizing a society for the advancement of collectors' interests and for the encouragement of the art. Those present at the meeting were: Reverend and Mrs. W. A. Brewer, Mr. and Mrs. E. J. Cross, Miss Sara M. Daly, Mr. G. H. Gihon, and Mr. Sheldon Cheney. These became charter members of the society."

Such was the opening paragraph of an article which related the account of the by-laws, organization, and constitution of the little society called the California Bookplate Society. The date is of special significance, for it was a year and a month after one of the major disasters of the United States, and it represented the founding of a society as well as the establishment of a bookplate publication which eventually became the official organ of the society. In November, 1906, had appeared the first number of *California Bookplates,* a magazine considered a rarity today. It was announced as "a little magazine devoted to bookplates in general and to Californian bookplates in particular, edited and issued occasionally by Sheldon Cheney, Berkeley, California." In the pages of this excellent publication appeared check lists, editorials, exchange lists, and

biographical sketches of ex libris subjects and personalities all over the world, as well as very authoritative pronouncements upon Californian bookplates and artists. The distinguished editor was the first student of ex libris to consider, in print at least, the value of the historic Californian plates. Committees of the society's members were appointed to begin a check list of such

plates to be incorporated in a survey similar in scope to that of *American Bookplates,* by Charles Dexter Allen.

That the magazine antedated the formation of the society is a tribute to the stricken community, a herald of the lively interest in the subject which has prevailed up to the present day. Those of us who find a sustaining and valuable satisfaction in our pursuit of any department of ex libris service should pay heed to

Sheldon Cheney and the coterie to which he belonged, as well as to the major collectors who have gathered well in this state.

The first exhibition of the California Bookplate Society was arranged by the members at the Century Club Hall in San Francisco on October 13, 1908. At that time it was the largest exhibition of bookplates ever held in the West.

The bookplate of the California Bookplate Society by Sheldon Cheney contains four of the historic plates of the state. A medallion of the beloved old Santa Barbara Mission appears in the center of the design and is framed by poppies. This society has another plate, a woodcut which was engraved by William Fowler Hopson and designed by Eleanor Plaw, an early artist member of the society.

To Olive Percival of Los Angeles falls the undivided honor of having the first exhibition of bookplates in Southern California in the clubhouse of the Friday Morning Club in March, 1911. A copy of this charming catalogue reads like a directory of Angeleños of a few decades ago and is, above all, a tribute to this scholarly collector whose collection bears the stamp of sound ex libris knowledge. To this exhibition Mary Eleanor Curran contributed extensively of her designs, thus supplementing the valuable collection of early American and "little masters" lent by Miss Percival.

The Bookplate Association International was organized by Helen Wheeler Bassett in Los Angeles in 1925, with eighteen charter members and twelve artist charter members. Truly international, this younger among ex libris organizations has more than justified its ambitious title, for the yearly exhibitions have been a Cook's tour for the Western members. They have been privileged to view entries from all corners of the earth—a veritable ex libris *esperanto,* illustrating most forcibly the far-reaching effects of a fifteenth-century invention, printing, as wedded to an age-old expression of the universal man, art. A phrase from the constitution seems to fit particularly well the notable achievements of this society: "to form a sustained medium of communication and cooperation between individuals everywhere who may be interested in bookplates."

The writer of this volume has often referred to membership in the Bookplate Association International as a passport to travel, for in her years of travel by correspondence and in the paths formed by the tangled tracks of exchanges, there has seemed no country too small to have at least a few ex libris collectors who are cordially disposed to unknown correspondents because of competitions in the Los Angeles society.

The first exhibition of the Bookplate Association International was held in the former Los Angeles Public Library, a fledgling event proudly attended by members and the curious public. The catalogues of the exhibition are listed among the ex libris publications in bibliographies and present an illuminating array of artists and owners of bookplates. The society has no official plate.

Four of the notable collections of the ex libris world and of California are those of the late Reverend

W. A. Brewer of Burlingame, now continued by Mrs. Brewer; of Katharine French Burnham and of Olive Percival of Los Angeles; and of Louise E. Winterburn of San Francisco.

The Brewer collection, which contains over seven thousand plates, is notable for proofs and rare plates of the group of ex libris designers of American "little masters," as well as the outstanding plates of Europe and America. The set of Edwin Davis French plates lacks only about thirty-five of being complete. Perhaps Dr. Brewer decided upon this early specialty because of his own plate by French and his friendship with the eminent artist. This plate, Brainerd 228, has as center interest the church of his father, the Reverend Alfred Lee Brewer, St. Matthew's Church in Burlingame. The old family home at Norwich, Connecticut, is at the top; the ivy so beautifully executed in the engraving typifying the birthplace of the family in England, from which it was transplanted; and the seal of the United States indicating the family's adopted country.

There is also a plate by William Edgar Fisher, in which St. Matthew's Church is adapted from the plate by French. Another plate is by William Fowler Hopson, a wood engraving which, by its wintry beauty, reminds us of the technique of Bewick.

The friendships of this beloved clergyman comprised most of the great names in ex libris tradition for a half century. A visit to the collection, housed in the memory-laden study which was presided over by this collector, is an experience of edification in its example of the industry expended upon a collection of historic and archive-like proportions. In the main, the
.(1 0 6).

collection of Dr. Brewer was formed during the years prior to 1915, when he was associated with his father at St. Matthew's School, of which he later became head master. No small part of the value of the collection lies in the exact cataloguing, grouping, and mounting of the plates, upon the backs of which have been written anecdotes, data, and information respecting the owners or the acquisition of the plates. The writer found extremely interesting the section of early typographicals of Californians, the notations regarding which could easily form the basis for a Domesday Book of Californians.

Katharine French Burnham is a name long known to collectors and one which has appeared in collectors' lists in several languages for over thirty-five years. The joint plate of the Burnhams by Edwin Davis French, Brainerd 213, has been the "open sesame" to garner treasures which have been the despair of the beginner. "Doctor, lawyer, merchant, chief," as well as the *haut monde* of the literary, the artistic, and the theatrical worlds seem to have trooped in their decorative array through her hospitable ex libris library upon the sober mounts of careful cataloguing. Mrs. Burnham also has a plate, designed by Adrian Feint, for her extensive library of dramatic books. The eminent Australian artist has achieved an extremely effective bookplate through his skilled balance of laurel wreath and masks of comedy and tragedy.

A visit to the Burnham treasures, which are housed in a library containing valuable literary ex libris contributions of many countries, is an incentive to collectors and a tribute to the methodical and devoted care of the lovable dean of collectors in Southern California. There are about three thousand plates in this collection, as well as innumerable brochures, pamphlets, and contributions to the subject; also an ex libris library

which contains ample resources from which research might be made in the preparation of any history of the subject. Among these volumes may be found check lists, rare ex libris memorials, and copies of limited editions, as well as volumes which are considered milestones in bookplate history.

The memory of the writer turns fondly to her first

ex libris friend in California, Olive Percival, who has been mentioned previously. The owner of thousands of plates, of which she herself has lost count, Miss Percival has extended her friendships to many continents through the possession of a large number of personal plates for exchange. She has striven for the individual and the beautiful in design, rather than the *outré*, costly, or rare; that is, if a choice were to be made. She once wrote: "Mere numbers do not appeal. All I cherish must be of some special interest, or show some beauty of design. Copper, engraved, or etched plates never seem to me so fitting as woodcuts; they are the orchids, the jewelry, among the different processes; one respects them, but they

do not seem to be of the fine old company made up of the Arts of the Book." As a result her collection is a veritable association group, with roots bearing into the eighteenth century, the nineties, the Edwardian, and the Georgian eras. The Ellen Terrys, Gordon Craigs, Wilbur Macey Stones, and Kate Greenaways comprise sections instead

.(1 0 9).

of the ones and twos of less fortunate collectors. Her generosity is inexhaustible, and her guiding hand has in no small measure been responsible for the lively and well-grounded knowledge of ex libris in the Southland. Though mounts and cardboard are legitimate housing for bookplates, Miss Percival further dignifies special favorites by framing; thus each tiny plate receives the emphasis which is perhaps denied it in more ordinary collections.

Miss Percival's array of personal ex libris reads like a *Who's Who* among ex libris artists, beginning with the E. H. New plate, said by many to be one of the really great names to grace the art since Dürer, Holbein, Bewick, and Bartolozzi. The artist of the New Loggan Series of Oxford Architectural Prints has shown his usual masterly simplicity and perfection of drawing in the American plate depicting the pre-Revolutionary homestead of the Percivals in the Berkshires. Miss Percival's plates also include the George Plank music marker and garden-book plates; the Jay Chambers dramatic plate; the Wilbur Macey Stone goldenrod plate; the gift plate and the juvenilia plate by Margaret Ely Webb; and the bunch-of-primroses, the bluebell, and the dwarf-pine-tree labels which she designed herself for use in the books of her girlhood and in brochures. Her collection of children's bookplates is perhaps the largest on the Pacific coast.

Louise E. Winterburn's collection contains several specialties other than the one for which she is famed: the bookplates of royalty. As president of the California Bookplate Society, she dispenses bountifully of her gracious favors, her home being a veritable Northern Californian Mecca for ex librists. Her ex libris guest book and scrap book of articles, clippings, testimonials, letters, and appreciations are original features, not the usual fact in the busy lives of collectors.

In addition to maintaining the above, she is compiling a manuscript copy of the history of the collection, its accessions, and contacts, which will contain ex libris chronicles of unequalled interest. Her collections are of great educational value, and as such play an important part in the cultural activities of San Francisco. It is notable that even such similar entities as collections possess definite characterizing notes; for the onlooker, viewing the magnificent group of bookplates of royalty, is bewildered by the display of pomp and circumstance, of orders and potentates, and feels as if he were attending a coronation ceremony.

The Winterburn collection is perhaps the largest of its kind in existence. It is believed to exceed that of the British Museum, which has a collection of bookplates of royalty bequeathed by the late Sir Augustus Wollaston Franks. Louise Winterburn began to specialize in 1927 at the suggestion of the late Reverend W. A. Brewer, personally obtaining a number of these extremely elusive plates. In 1933 she acquired the collection of Richard Edwin Thomas, of Beeleigh Abbey, Essex, England. At present she owns plates of royalty from twenty countries, a list of which is on file in the Library of Congress, Washington, D. C. Her own plate is an etching by Dorothy Payne in which the titles of a group of volumes reveal the ex libris specialties of the owner: Badeley, Downey, Barrett, French and others.

To the collecting of plates of Californians, the writer has devoted the past three years, the result being

.(1 1 1).

that her collection is believed to be the largest group
concerned with a given locality in the ex libris world.
While such a grouping is not the usual method in the
classification of bookplates, it possesses interest for
the owner who gathers information of an historical and

biographical nature regarding plates and their owners,
the whole forming a body of information for reference and record. The more orthodox listings are those
in which the artist is detailed, together with the ex
libris classifications, countries, dates, or other speciali-
zations as desired by the compiler.

.(1 1 2).

The writer owns a number of personal plates, among which the yucca plate has already been described. The *Isola San Giorgio* plate was cut on wood by Victor Stuyvaert of Belgium, and represents Venice at the time of Aldus Manutius. She also cherishes two typographical plates, one by Ruth Thomson Saunders and the other by Ward Ritchie. There are two sizes of the Brandenburg plate, so called because the famous first bookplate found in the Carthusian Monastery of Buxheim, Suabia, forms the center of the plate. This plate is used solely for marking books about bookplates. It was designed by Maxwell Hamilton Noll, and a few copies have been hand colored by the artist in pigments approximating those of the famous ex libris *incunable* of the fifteenth century. For books and pamphlets the writer uses a philatelic rarity which will remain unlisted by the Bureau of Engraving and Printing. This tiny bookplate, the size of the recent National Park issue, was cut on linoleum by Angela S. Crispin and printed by the artist in red, violet, and black. In its small space may be clearly seen *El Camino Real,* so appropriate in relation to the owner's present ex libris specialization.

Edith Emerson Spencer's collection is characterized by bookplates of distinguished artists and of artistic charm. Her own ex libris are fine examples of the art. The exquisite hand-illuminated *Horae Beatae* plate was adapted by Maxwell Hamilton Noll from a *Book of Hours* of the fifteenth century, and is radiantly colorful in the mediaeval style.

Geraldine T. Kelly possesses a bookplate by the gifted Margaret Ely Webb. It is with all the pleasure of discovering a key to a cipher that we learn that the

.(1 1 4).

tiny rose on the name ribbon is a floral canting device for the owner's middle name, Tudor. Miss Kelly also uses a tiny Tudor rose plate, which is a linoleum cut by Angela S. Crispin, for marking smaller books and pamphlets.

In the Frances Dallam Moss bookplate by Margaret Ely Webb, a graceful Renaissance lady walks in a garden at twilight. Below in the flowered border of the design is a line from one of Shakespeare's sonnets: *That thereby beauty's rose might never die.* The tiny angels symbolize music and writing.

Muriel Alderman, Marian Dassonville, Katharine F. Ball, and Christine Price have interesting collections which the writer hopes to visit in the future. Clare Montgomery's gargoyle of Notre Dame, etched by Ella Dwyer of Australia, has proved as able a courier as his witty owner. Miss Montgomery owns a notable collection of general ex libris artists, as well as an unusually complete list of the designs of the late Franz Marquis von Bayros. She has also amassed a fine group of the bookplates of D. Y. Cameron.

Eleanor Homer and Helen Mooney Fenton are names encountered in all gatherings of ex libris enthusiasts, and they own splendid collections. Each has an engraved bookplate by James Webb, showing a characteristic Californian landscape. Grace Webster Wickes' collection is well rounded, but she especially favors her ex libris correspondence and anecdotes gathered while she was garnering her treasures. Greta Rowell owns three ex libris: one an engraved plate by John W. Jameson another by C. K. Berryman. and one designed by herself. Her collection contains many treasures. Leota Woy's collection forms the basis for ex libris lectures. Her own plate is reproduced in the Artists' chapter, as are also the plates of other collector-artists: Ruth Thomson Saunders, Maxwell Hamilton Noll, and Margaret Ely Webb.

D. L. Bogardus of the Department of Bindings of the Henry E. Huntington Library owns a unique collection of leather ex libris, the first of that specialization to be noted by the writer. Eric Ellert's plate was designed by Axel Nugaard, and represents an ancient dolmen of Scandinavia. His Hogarth plate is a treasure envied by many collectors.
Other Californian bibliophiles who possess bookplate collections are Albert M. Bender, Samuel T. Farquhar, John Howell, Major Harry Dravo Parkin, the late Orra E. Monnette, Thomas Wayne Norris, Dr. Rathbone, Dr. Crispin, and Dr. Potter.

The University of California owns a notable collection of plates, of which Joseph C. Rowell, librarian emeritus and archivist, has taken charge and arranged exhibitions at intervals. The University of California at Los Angeles has recently been presented with one of the most remarkable collections of bookplates in the ex libris world. This gift of the Bookplate Association International contains over four thousand uniformly mounted items, the result of the yearly exhibitions already mentioned. A veritable panorama of contemporary as well as past trends in ex libris history has thus been gathered, for competing artists added extra plates to enrich this collection. Grouped by countries, these plates are readily accessible, and present possibilities for study of processes, styles, and international characteristics. The State Library at Sacramento, Mills College, Stanford University, the University of Southern California, and the Los Angeles Public Library are among other public institutions maintaining collections and welcoming exchanges.

The zeal of collectors of bookplates in California is of an amazing quality and is equalled only by the longevity of their endeavor and the range of their targets. We have noted that new societies and publications have been the fact of ex libris history in California; yet the collectors themselves antedate the turn of the century, and their activities are continuing without abatement at the present time. Aside from the official exhibitions of societies, private exhibits are much in demand, either by schools, clubs, or museums.

Despite over thrice ten alarmingly active collectors, their orbits do not seem to coincide. Verily they must be governed by a traffic system comparable to that of the celestial spheres, for by some sort of *noblesse oblige* the collector traffic lanes are left clear. Animated by the common bond of ex libris, many students, writers, lecturers, artists, and bibliographers in the state add to their other talents the duties and the privileges of collectors, and to that end have they allied themselves with the collector marts of the world.

.(1 1 7).

Chapter IX

BOOKPLATES OF DOCTORS

"De médico, poeta, y loco,
Todos tenemos un poco." *

TO the Cross and the Crown we might justly add the *caduceus,* for this symbol of medical ministrations to mankind deserves mention in the history of the beginnings of civilization in any locality. This is equally true of California, for from the earliest days physicians have played as prominent a part in the cultural activities as in the exercise of their profession. From Pedro Prat, surgeon of the royal squadron of the *San Cárlos,* to the present day, we find mention of medical men, their writings both general and technical, their libraries, and of course their bookplates. This subject of medical bookplates is an extensive one, for a complete history would include plates of hospitals, gift bequests, endowments, personal libraries, school and college libraries, as well as the many ex libris intended by physicians for personal use. One might expect the *caduceus* and the staff of Aesculapius to be the dominant artistic symbol, but as a class these medical plates exhibit an endless and pleasing variety.

Pedro Prat, described by Father Engelhardt as "faithful Pedro Prat," was present at San Diego on July 16, 1769, when the Cross was erected. He is mentioned with affection in many of the letters of Father Serra and in the diary of Captain Vicente Villa of the *San Cárlos*. What an interesting item his bookplate would have been!

In fact, honors for the earliest medical ministrator are divided. In the search for what might have been the earliest physician—not to mention his book or book-plate—Juan Antonio Coronel, *arriero* of the land expedition which was led by Portolá and Serra, intruded his unacademic appearance even before Señor Prat. While he has escaped much historic mention, the muleteer's treatment of the *padre presidente* will always be an interesting story.

The forty-six-day journey by foot from Sonora in Mexico had proved serious for Father Serra's leg ulcer, which had resulted from a cactus wound during his first year in Baja California. When the journey was well advanced, the ulcer became so painful that he was forced to be carried on a litter. Prostrated with pain and unable to sleep, he was implored by Governor Portolá to return to Loreto, but the magnificent missionary, at last upon the threshold of his life's work, refused with the iron determination that was to be responsible for his later successes.

According to the story, Serra called the *arriero* and asked, "Son, canst thou make me a remedy for the ulcer on my foot and leg?"

"*Padre,*" answered the muleteer, "what can I know? Am I a surgeon? I am an *arriero* and have healed only the sores of beasts."

"Then, son, suppose me a beast and this ulcer a saddle gall. And make for me the medicament thou wouldst apply to a beast."

.(1 1 9).

Thereupon this muleteer, the first of his calling to achieve historic mention, mixed tallow and herbs, heated the mixture, and applied it like a poultice. The pain lessening, Serra continued the journey, but never was he to be free from this earthly annoyance. It is edifying to note that in his first letter from Alta California, written on July 3, 1769, to Father Lector Francisco Palóu at San Fernando College in Mexico City, he refers briefly to this incident of the journey: "In fact, it was not worth mentioning."

What a triumph for the ex libris searcher it would be to find the plate of Felix Wierzbicki, the Polish physician of San Francisco and author of the first descriptive book to be written in English in that city! *California As It Is And As It May Be,* published in 1849, is a curious compendium of medical information, stage guidebook, geological handbook, and such advice as this to miners: "Wherever there is oak, there is apt to be gold; when oak gives place to pine, quartz pinches out."

Another bookplate of importance would be that of Dr. Cephas Bard of Ventura, who wrote a rare pamphlet, also one of the book "finds" of the state. An address read before a meeting of the Southern California Medical Society at San Diego in 1894, it gave an account of the methods, medicaments, superstitions, and instruments used by the Californian Indians and the early Spaniards. *A Contribution to the History of Medicine in Southern California* is a valuable narrative as thrilling as fiction, for it brings to our minds the insuperable difficulties endured by the early *padres* and explorers, who must have found volumes like Florilegio's *Medicinal* provokingly inadequate.

.(1 2 0).

The report of this fruitless search is shared with ex libris collector-doctors in the hope that they may unearth these elusive bookplates. A clue, however, was supplied through a survey of *California Medicine,* by John Shuman, in which several plates in the writer's own collection sprang to life from their lethargy in the section assigned to exchangeable duplicates.

Dr. Walter Lindley, a prominent pioneer physician of Los Angeles, was active in educational and civic affairs of the state. His plate represents his home and literary interests in the charming device of mission bells. Though it was designed by C. Valentine Kirby as late as 1910, it signifies by the date 1873 the inception of a career of distinguished service.

.(1 2 1).

H. Bert Ellis' ornamental signature adorns a plate in which an owl, a bookcase, scrolls, skull and cross-bones, together with fraternal symbols, embellish an entirely personal design. Reading through stories of Davila, Soler, and Quixano of the Spanish period, and of Den, Marsh, and Keith of the American period, we arrive at a list of the first graduates of the University of Southern California and find that H. Bert Ellis was a member of the class of 1888. This forms no clue as to the certainty of the ex libris date, but it is at least an approximation. Until future claimants arise, I shall believe Dr. Ellis' bookplate to be the first medical ex libris in Los Angeles.

The medical history of San Francisco begins with Dr. John Townsend, who hung out the first medical shingle in Northern California in 1846. He was aide to Captain Sutter and surgeon in the Micheltorena campaign. At the beginning of the gold rush, physicians flocked to the diggings. Among them was Dr. Fayette Clappe, the husband of "Dame Shirley," the delightful letter writer. He was one of the first medical practitioners at Rich Bar on the Feather River in 1849. Within a few weeks after his arrival, there were no less than twenty-nine physicians in that busy locality.

These names are offered for suggestions in future ex libris hunts and as incidents of investigation, but a perusal of the old medical histories will repay anyone. The quaint observations and human interpolations are historically valuable as well as humorous.

The earliest dated physician's bookplate of our century is that of Dr. Homer Clifton Oatman, which was drawn in 1901 by Arthur Wellington Clarke. Long known

.(1 2 2).

to ex libris collectors, Clarke is now revealed as a doctor-artist. Conspicuously lacking in the signs of the profession, this delightful one-hoss-shay bookplate utilizes a theme known to the schoolboy. The bewigged and literary doctor pursues a leisurely course to his patient, but one fears that the doctor's kit may bump beneath the wheels, so intently does he scan the volume.

A name connected with magnificent benefactions to Californian education as well as to medicine is that of the late Norman Bridge. Although no medical symbols appear on his bookplate, it illustrates the phase of his early life as a plowboy in New England which he asked the artist, A. N. Macdonald, to use as design feature.

The collection of early medical books of the late LeRoy Crummer is of worldwide fame. They are marked by a bookplate which is an adaptation of an illustration in a sixteenth-century book, *Shyp of Folys*. A woodcut of a mediaeval physician drawn by Arthur J. Brown, it is admirably fitted for the rarities it adorns. A learned man in a cell of monastic features contemplates the wonders of science in the marvellous age in which he lives, in all probability bewailing, then as now, the lack of importance placed by the laity upon research.

Carl Oscar Borg's design for the bookplate of C. J. Cresmer possesses something of a mural breadth, for what appears to be a well of learning was interpreted by Mr. Borg as the ancient rite of divination by smoke. The figure reverently reading before the altar is outlined against a Druidic grove of classic mystery.

An alarmingly alive *caduceus* is held by a beautifully modelled Hippocrates in Elwyn H. Welch's plate. The vividness of Ruth Thomson Saunders' characteristic medium also appears on the joint plate of Arthur and Katharine Weber. That John Cree Wilson and William Louis Weber retire to the High Sierra and the desert to seek surcease from professional strain is suggested by their bookplates. The Wilson plate, which is a wood-cut by Franz Geritz, indicates by a majestic stag the owner's interest in hunting.

Norman H. Williams' plate by Leota Woy shows the historic Williams home through an archway of rose trees. The physician's interest in books and music is also indicated. Rawson J. Pickard introduces a symbol which may be unfamiliar to the laity, for his plate uses the winged bull of St. Luke, patron saint of physicians. Also it suggests the interest in Gothic architecture which he shares with his wife. The plate shows a date palm which shadowed the home in which they lived at Colon Hospital. A quotation from Rabelais' *Abbey of Thélème* completes a strikingly original bookplate, which was engraved by Henri Bouvier of Paris.

New Zealand symbols are found in the E. Ross Jenney plate, the central portion containing the *tiki* of native mythology, which, together with the hemispheres, denotes the owner's interest in travel. The symbols in the upper left and right signify, respectively, the *raki* and *ura* of Maori lore.

Mildred Bryant Brooks has etched a notable composition for W. Curtis Brigham, whose love of books, the out of doors, and hunting are represented in his plate. From the leaded windows of his library wings a flight of geese, also suggesting the freedom of knowledge—the flight of thought. The joint plate of Morris and Anne Slemons is noncommittal as to their bibliographical activities; yet the Rockwell Kent design suggests their unity of tastes, which has resulted in an outstanding collection of first editions, autographed and

.(1 2 5).

rare books. Another blend of interests is indicated in the plate for rare books designed by Angela S. Crispin for Dr. Egerton Crispin, who also collects bookplates, specializing in medical plates. His plate has skillfully combined varied design elements: the Celtic border was derived from designs found in a volume entitled,

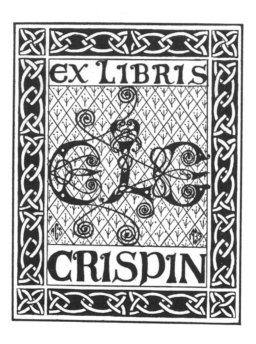

The Art of Illuminating as Practiced in Europe from the Earliest Times; and the lettering, contributing a stained-glass effect, was adapted from the Cottonian manuscript, Vespasian A 1, found in the Scriptorium of the Augustinian Monastery in Kent and now in the British Museum.

The bookplate of Millbank Johnson places a mission imaginatively beside the sea, impairing not a whit the composition in which palms, mountains, and eucalyptus trees form a design replete with Californian symbols. The plate was the work of James Webb.

Junius Cravens has accomplished a skillful blending of objects for Emma K. Willits, who has been connected with the Children's Hospital at San Francisco for many years. The oak tree in the center is an exact drawing of a favorite tree shadowing *Casa del Esedra,* her home in Palo Alto. Beyond the circular seat that gives its name to the home may be glimpsed San Francisco Bay. The medical symbol is superimposed upon a Della Robbia semi-lune of the Children's Hospital, itself adapted from the Foundling Hospital in Florence. The frame of the design is a section of the pillars of the doorway to the hospital.

The joint plate of Rene and Robert Legge is a reminiscent symbol, for much of their work in Northern California was done in sight of Mt. Shasta. Who knows but that the Gerbode bookplate may be even more historic than merely an ex libris satisfactory to the owner? In the

.(1 2 7).

plate of Frank Leven Albert Gerbode, experiments are being carried on with boxes and lights to ensnare the dull-witted cat, thereby glorifying the intelligent one.

Dr. J. Roy Jones' plate by Theodore Baggleman has for its design feature the saddlebags containing the original bottles used by Dr. E. W. Bathurst of Siskiyou County in the early seventies. The bookplate of Max Dunievitz contains symbols of medical significance by

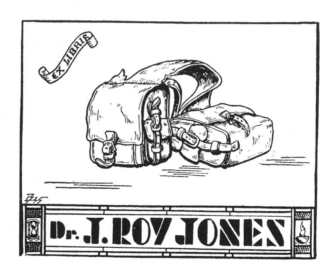

using instruments, college seal, busts of Aesculapius and Hippocrates, and the indispensable volumes of a physician's library. Pipe and chessmen constitute avocations, but the derisive fish, leaping from a lake, bespeak an honest fisherman; for the owner and the artist, Rudolph S. E. Dogge, once took a fishing trip during which no fish were caught. The bookplate of Josephine and Easton Lum, with its motto, *Lang may your lum reek,* implies that their name is the Scottish word for chimney.

In an unusually interesting plate, Wallace Irving Terry of the University of California incorporates the seal of Berkeley with a view from his library toward the Sausalito shore of San Francisco Bay. Dr. Benteen

of the same university has an etched plate by K. Hyde. Philip King-Brown's plate has an extremely fine view of Santa Barbara Mission, with a bust of Hippocrates to remind us of the owner's profession. The specialization of Dr. Adelaide Brown is unmistakably proved by the feathered biped on her bookplate. The plate of Forrest Anderson is almost a lesson in neurology, for the specialty of the owner is indicated by the brain, cord, ganglion, and other features of the vegetative and central nervous system. These have been utilized by James Ashbaugh as artistic elements in the design.

Quite as unique is the plate of Dr. Lawrence Hobbs Acres, in which the design is a seal of wax imprinted by a signet ring used by the Fourth Earl of Chesterfield as a seal. Dr. Acres writes that he made one hundred impressions in wax before he obtained a blob which could be used in photogravure etching. The fourth Earl was not an ancestor, as at first sight might be supposed, but employed as his barrister Dr. Acres' many times great-grandfather. "While the head should have been that of Hippocrates instead of Socrates for a physician, still it would not have had the significance for me," the owner confided as he related incidents in the building of the plate, which was executed by Joseph Love of an engraving firm.

The armorial bookplate has ever been the favorite of the medical profession, and this is especially true of Californian plates. One of the earliest medical bookplates is the richly colored armorial of Wesley Wilbur Beckett, which though signed in his own writing yet bears the family surname of the à Beckett family. The *caduceus* is noted in many heraldic plates where it may be inserted almost to obscurity on account of its decorative quality as well as its medical associations.

Dr. Visscher, Robert Rathbone, Arthur Bond Cecil, and Frank Wadsworth Chandler have armorials by James Webb. The armorial of Edward Marshall Pallette was

.(1 3 0).

designed by Carleton Winslow. Alfred E. Banks, George Washington McCoy, and Henry William Mills are other owners of armorial bookplates.

Robert Rathbone and Edwin Potter are both collector-doctors, the former having a general collection in which

Robert Rathbone, M.D.

he exchanges his armorial plate engraved by James Webb, while **Dr.** Potter has three major collections as well as his specialization in early American, symbolic-medical, Sidney L. Smith, and an almost complete set of Edwin Davis French plates. In the early American group Dr. Potter possesses not a few unknown to the earlier authorities, and his own ex libris are fine examples of the art. His Chippendale armorial was designed by himself, suggested in part, as he says, after "Henry Dawkins, who borrowed as well, for he was accused, probably unjustly, of making continental money." Dr. Potter's description of the plate thus recalls one of the less pleasant incidents in the history of early American ex libris. The bookplate was engraved for him by James Fincken. He also owns a plate by Sidney L. Smith, listed as number 166 in the Smith check list.

Chapter X

BOOKPLATES OF HOTELS, CLUBS,
AND ASSOCIATIONS

"The question of a name was settled by the non-
commissioned officers of the *Portsmouth,* who told
Brown that they would make and paint the sign if
he would call his hotel the Portsmouth House. The
sign was carefully finished, brought ashore, and
put up, the first signboard in Yerba Buena."
—Catherine Coffin Phillips. *

THE bookplate of the Society of California Pioneers
approximates an al fresco treatment of state history, for from the *San Cárlos* to the Pony
Express, it depicts that which could belong to no other
state or group. The artist, Louise Thian Diamond, has
cunningly contrived to suggest by her skill in perspective
a chronological sequence of events in its minute space.
These same figures appear on the certificate of the Society
of California Pioneers.

This society, located at 5 Pioneer Place, San Francisco, is engaged in collecting and preserving data and
history of California and the Pacific coast. Its own
history dates from August 31, 1850, when the steamer
California arrived with news of the death of Zachary
Taylor. A meeting was called by John W. Geary to ar-
range for a demonstration to the memory of the President. Argonauts up to that time had been more or less

.(1 3 2).

dissociated, but the plans for the obsequies were per-
fected by a group of "old residents," Samuel Brannan,
William D. M. Howard, J. C. L. Wadsworth, Talbot

Green, and Benjamin S. Lippincott. From this group
grew the society today so active, which even from the first
included two classes of members: first, those who were
residents of the state prior to January 1, 1849; and

second, those who were residents prior to January 1, 1850, and the male descendants of both groups. Further account of the members of this society would supply readers with events of utmost importance to the state, and their collected writings and individual experiences would constitute a Californian *Who's Who*.

There is also a plate found in the historic Stockton section, a typographical for the library of the San Joaquín Society of Pioneers at Stockton, a society founded in 1868.

Bohemian Club

CLASS _____

ACC _____

The plate of the Bohemian Club, one of San Francisco's beloved traditions, contains a quotation from *Midsummer Night's Dream*. It reminds us of the annual and equally famous festival held in the Bohemian Grove. The design is the coat of arms adopted by the club in 1873, upon which appear as armorial achievements the delightful implements of the arts and the muses. The bookplate was designed by G. J. Denny, a marine painter and a member of the club.

The Francisca Club plate was designed by Fannie W. Delahanty in 1907 and is delightful with its view of the Church of St. Francis of Assisi. The Pacific Union Club on Nob Hill uses an engraved plate, the fraternal

.(1 3 4).

dwelling having been the home of James C. Flood. This colorful miner had for neighbors three gentlemen of equal fame, Collis P. Huntington, Leland Stanford, and Charles Crocker. Near them, on the site of the present Fairmont Hotel, lived James G. Fair, of Comstock Lode fame. It was this group of nabobs which gave the name Nob Hill to that section for its reflection of the glories of the Diamond Jim Brady era.

Caravanserics of charm and memory to travellers who have sojourned therein are the hotels which own bookplates. Miramar Hotel's plate was designed by Tom Mills. The Margaret Baylor Inn presents a fiesta scene reminding visitors of Santa Barbara's yearly festival which invokes the past in unique manner. The outside world is challenged to produce a similar fête, in which the townspeople don *mantilla* and *caballero* costumes each year, not only for pageant and ball, but for the prosaic discharge of daily duty. The Squirrel Inn plate, which will remind Angeleños of pleasant associations, was designed by Mrs. W. H. Burnham. It shows a representation of the original inn, which has been replaced with another edifice.

The University Club of Los Angeles has a bookplate designed by August Bissiri in tones of brown and sepia. A figure clad in doublet and jerkin is sitting in the sconce of a mission bell tower, through which one can glimpse a wave-washed silvery beach. The bookplate of the University Club of Pasadena, which suggests the missions and landscapes of California, was designed by Dr. Charles H. Benjamin.

The bookplate of the Art Study Club of Santa Barbara, which is used to mark gifts from members, was designed by Margaret Ely Webb. In it an unfinished sketch and an exquisitely arranged bouquet betray the occupations of the members. The same artist has made a plate for the San Foca Garden Guild.

Loren Barton's plate for the Women's Athletic Club of Los Angeles reflects the charm and the old Italian feeling of the court outside the Margaret Robertson Memorial Library. The plate of the Women's City Club of Berkeley might be an illustration from an incunabulum.

for a stout dame and her children are pulling proof to aid Mijnheer Husband in his mediaeval print shop. W. A. Paxson designed a plate for the Friday Morning Club of Los Angeles, in which the façade of the modern

SOUTHERN CALIFORNIA
WOMAN'S PRESS CLUB

clubhouse might resemble a Greek temple to accompany the Aspasia-like figure in the foreground. The Southern California Woman's Press Club has a pictorial plate by Leota Woy, in which sundry writers' devices are heraldically simulated beneath a prancing Pegasus.

.(1 3 7).

There are two mercantile institutions which have achieved notable plates. The California and Hawaiian Sugar Refining Company of San Francisco has a bookplate by John Henry Nash; and the S. and G. Gump Company has chosen a plate as applicable to its commercial activity as to the mighty city of which it is so characteristic an institution. The portals of a magnificent iron gate open upon a globe which centers the Western hemisphere, set in Balboa's ocean beneath a sunlit sky. The gateway to the left enshrines a medallion figure of Buddha, swinging toward the Orient; and the head of a Greek god typifies the glory that was Greece—the Occident as it faces the Europe of antiquity. The bookplate might be a pictorial translation of Herbert E. Bolton's description of San Francisco: "A link between the restless Occident and the patient, mighty Orient."

The Izaac Waltons of a southern shore have a fellow member who is, incidentally, a writer; we're certain that Zane Grey would not object to the reversal of emphasis upon his talents. The plate of the Tuna Club of Avalon, Santa Catalina Island, is described by Daniel B. Fearing, the authority on angling plates, as containing "a tuna, tuna rod, reel, line, and gaff hook, as well as the Tuna Club button." Fearing lists this plate as number 278.

Francis William Vreeland has designed a plate for the Daughters of the American Revolution, in which their emblem upon a distaff is set beneath a ferocious bear. The vertical section of a golden poppy reminds us that one of the society chapters is named for this flower. The grizzly bear, the state symbol, was adopted as the chief figure of the state coat of arms in 1850; hence its frequent appearance in the ex libris of California.

.(1 3 8).

.(1 3 9).

Río Oso, Cañada de los Osos, and *Ositas* are Spanish variations of the idea and indicate geographical points thus named by the missionary fathers who were prone to

confer upon localities names which were often humorous or suggestive of incidents or of surrounding features. Bears were very common in the early days of California. The Bear Flag Rebellion of 1846, following the declaration of war between Mexico and the United States, was a brief incident. It ended when Commodore John D. Sloat took possession of California for the United States, but the flag was adopted as the state flag by legislative enactment on February 3, 1911.

Searches into old Californian books often reveal volumes from fraternal organizations. The hand-stamp of the Odd Fellows was noticed in a copy of B. E. Lloyd's *Lights and Shades of San Francisco*. Obviously these hand-stamps do not find their way into bookplate collections, but they are important chiefly for their age and bibliographical value. There are many Masonic bookplates older than those in use in the contemporary Masonic libraries throughout the state, and the writer is particularly anxious to learn of any plates which may be found in volumes of an early day. The wealth of symbolism which this organization contains affords the artist varied design elements. The plate illustrated is that of the Scottish Rite Library of Los Angeles.

Chapter XI

BOOKPLATES OF LIBRARIES AND LIBRARIANS

"For out of the old feldes, as men saythe,
Cometh al this newe corne fro yere to yere,
And out of olde bokes, in good faythe,
Cometh al this newe science that men lere."
—Geoffrey Chaucer. *

A MONG bookplate collectors, the complaint is often voiced that interest in library plates is lacking, and that the abstract themes sometimes used present to collectors an unfruitful field. Having voiced the same complaint in the past, the writer wishes to give tribute, as a sort of balm of Gilead, to the services rendered to this compilation which could have been completed by no other means than the library plate. If this section has been woefully impoverished, it is because such plates have been commandeered to enrich the opening chapter; for in the preservation of historical data in California the ex libris has been one of the most active agents. Although it is to be deplored that the printed label, the institutional design, and the inartistic sketch so often adorn the literary treasures of our libraries, it is recognized that funds are ever inadequate for books, let alone for their extra adornment.

Therefore it is with double interest that we glance through the array of library plates and marvel at the fund of accurate and valuable information therein enshrined. The initial office of utility need not be without charm. Certainly there is no locality in California in which some incident of its storied past might not fittingly be sketched by local artists. As a suggestion for our library boards, which are undoubtedly one of the cultural forces of the state, let this historizing influence be considered for the future, and let the literary aspect be expanded to embrace an artistic mission as well.

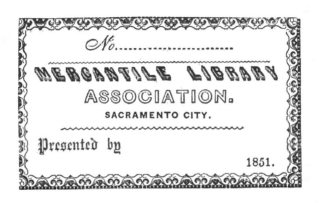

The earliest label of the State Library at Sacramento bears the name, B. B. Redding, State Printer. As Mr. Redding held this office from 1854 till 1855, the probable date of this plate is 1854. The earliest dated literary library plate is that of the Mercantile Library Association of Sacramento in 1851, a typographical presentation plate printed on yellow paper. Unhappily this library was a private project, and having but scant resources, it lived but slightly longer than its first year.

The plates of the Sutro Library are rich in historic

.(1 4 3).

lore and are as revealing of the famous landmarks as a
Currier and Ives might be. In the extreme left are the
Seal Rocks, nearer the center is the celebrated Cliff
House, and beneath the motto, *Labor omnia vincit,* are
Sutro Heights, Sutro Baths, the Naval Observatory, and
other municipal endowments of Adolph Sutro. Of great-
est value is the extremely clear delineation of the
Sutro Tunnel in the Comstock silver mines of Nevada.

In 1859, Sutro, the originator of this daring feat of
engineering, attempted a transverse tunnel to drain
the seven spurs of the famous Comstock Lode. The plate
is an exquisite piece of old engraving. Its source is
unknown, but the design indicates the presence of first-
rate artisans in this craft in the early days of San
Francisco. Had they but signed their plates, they might
have enjoyed the tribute justly their due, as well as

supplied bibliographical links to later students. Two
other varieties of this plate are to be found, with the
signature, *Moss del(ineavit)*. Also there is a colored
representation of the earlier plate. Very possibly the

artist was George Moss, who for many years was the librarian of the Sutro Library.

The Monterey Library possesses early associations,
giving us a glimpse of the first custom house in California and reminding us of other famous "firsts" in

connection with this city of "oaks of prodigious size," to quote from Vizcaíno's report to the Viceroy of Mexico. Monterey enshrined California's mother mission where lived the founder and where he lies buried. Here was her first custom house, with Thomas O. Larkin as first American consul. Here was the first presidio established by Portolá. Here was the first newspaper, *The Californian,* as well as the first printing press, that of Augustín Vicente Zamorano. And here was California's first theater. The typical cypress and the glorious bay complete the Monterey bookplate, which was designed by Cornelis Botke.

The Los Angeles Public Library owns an array of creditable bookplates, the most historic among them being the lovable but absurd angel plate. A careening angel with torch of learning and palm fronds of the tropical city, *Nuestra Señora la Reina de los Angeles de la Porciúncula,* wings benevolently over the city, upon which shines an effulgent sun. The angel might be the lady in a magician's act, so curiously is her suspension indicated; or perhaps the palm fronds are ailerons to supplement the seraphic wings. But pause, impious ex librists, before jesting at this flame-colored plate, for an unknown but reverent member of the library bookplate committee asked P. Doré, a local artist and wood engraver, to design and create a bookplate for the Los Angeles Library. This artist adapted the angel design from an illustration in the *Purgatorio* of his famous cousin, Paul Gustave Doré.

Although exact data could not be obtained on this design, several sources were approached for further details. Miss Mary Foy, the city's first salaried li-

brarian, said when consulted: "It probably came in with
Mr. Lummis, who was very much interested in bookplates.
I worked with him as secretary of the Southwest Museum,
and he had such a feeling for the historic values that he
reported everything with future generations in mind."

Olive Percival, long conversant with things artistic
in the Southland, recalls that P. Doré, a very old man,
had a wood-engraving shop near First and Broadway in
Los Angeles about 1891. As that era was the beginning
of the now familiar zinc and photoelectric methods of
illustration, the art of M. Doré languished. No other

.(1 4 7).

examples of his work are known to the writer. Since he died about 1892, this plate is thought to be one of the earliest ex libris in Los Angeles. Additional value is lent to the plate because of an authentic view of the metropolis-to-be which appears in the foreground.

The Los Angeles Library owns an interesting plate for the Francis Forrest Clark shorthand collection; the Ruth Thomson Saunders plate for the Jaroslaw de Zielinski music collection; and the Alfred Hammerbeck design for the Musicians' Fund collection. The official black and sepia plate for general books was designed by Norman Kennedy. It was in the Los Angeles Public Library that the first exhibition of the Bookplate Association International was held, as well as several of the later exhibits. Hence this association accords the library a great deal of gratitude for its patronage in fostering the art of ex libris.

The San Francisco Public Library plate was designed by Albertine Randall Wheelan and uses the legend of the phoenix as typifying the history of that intrepid city. From the burning book rises this bird of immortality, echoing the theme of the city seal. The Pasadena Public Library uses the symbol of the Crown City with a design of pine and dogwood. The California State Library uses printed labels for bequests and departmental labels. The Frances Schirmer Otto Memorial plate for the Santa Barbara Library resembles an old incunabulum illustration and was done by Edward B. Edwards. The La Jolla Public Library has two plates designed by W. J. Fenn.

The Mechanics' Mercantile Library on Post Street in San Francisco has a plate designed by Arthur F. Matthews, suggestive of the construction and building

.(1 4 8).

activities going on after the earthquake and fire of 1906. The Mercantile Library Association of San Francisco, which was organized in 1852, at first used a hand-stamp

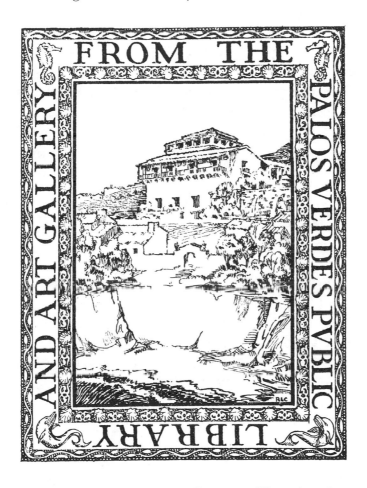

and later a printed label. The two libraries, however, must not be confused.

The Palos Verdes Public Library fulfills a double purpose in the community by being an art gallery as

.(1 4 9).

well. Its bookplate at first glance might seem a Zuñi pueblo or prehistoric dwelling because of the steep steps rising to set-back stories. But calm inspection reveals the wave-fringed beach, cliffs, and balconied library which typify, as Charles Cheney explains, "sea life for a community beside the sea, with the library building in the background." A border of dolphins, sea horses, shells, and sea weed completes a most attractive bookplate. It was designed by Ronald Campbell.

The Henry E. Huntington Library uses several typographical labels, variants which include donations and bequests, as well as photostatic reproductions of rare books, of which this library has an ever increasing number. To date these are: Reproduced from the British Museum Copy; Reproduced from the Bodleian Library Copy; Reproduced from the Henry E. Huntington Library Copy; and Henry E. Huntington Library. The inclusion of these plates serves to remind readers of this magnificent institution of worldwide fame, for the description of but a single section of its treasures would demand more detailed treatment.

The Library is only one part of the entire Henry E. Huntington Library and Art Gallery, which were the gift to the people of California of the late Henry Edwards Huntington, on whose death in May, 1927, the institution passed into the control of a self-perpetuating board of trustees. Situated in the center of the little city of San Marino on the edge of Pasadena, its fine botanical gardens provide a beautiful setting for the library building as well as that housing the founder's famous art collections. Dedicated to promoting the cause of research, the library's collections are composed mainly of English and American history and literature, with a remarkable assemblage of incunabula serving as a background for the study of continental influences on the rise of English culture. Mr. Huntington's extensive purchases of complete libraries and collections from 1911 to 1927, among which were numbered those of Frederick R. Halsey, E. Dwight Church, Beverly Chew, and the Earl of Ellesmere, were the basis of the present collection numbering approximately 210,000 volumes of printed material and 800,000 items of manuscripts and archives.

The Lassen County Library has preserved the first and only remaining pioneer house in that county, a building which has in turn been a hotel and a fortress. The monument illustrated is the one placed over Peter Lassen's grave, and was carved by an old pioneer. The only active volcano in continental United States, Mt. Lassen was named for Peter Lassen, who was born in 1800 in Copenhagen, Denmark. From Edwin A. Sherman's *Fifty Years of Masonry,* we learn of the part played by this hardy pioneer in the history of that organization in California. Before the discovery of gold, Lassen brought the first Masonic charter to the state, which was then under Mexican rule. He was prominent in the early affairs of the pioneer locality, and when a name for the county was selected in 1863, the choice fell unanimously on the heroic Peter Lassen. The tree on the spot where this pioneer asked to be buried is commemorated in the bookplate designed by Elsmore Lake. The figures on the stone are those which were carved on the monument over the grave of William Weatherlow, an early Indian fighter. Of this historic bookplate, Lenala Martin has written: "The last Indian massacre in that county was in 1868, which was, after all, not so long ago."

The libraries of Alameda, Butte, Colusa, Fresno, Merced, Madera, Kings, Monterey, Siskiyou, Stanislaus, and

Ventura counties have bookplates in which historical incidents and items of local color have been interwoven. Elsmore Lake has designed a number of these plates. To his artistic efforts is due the fact that many of the bookplates of county libraries in California possess to

a notable degree historic associations tastefully incorporated as ex libris. Often the typical industries and products of the state have been included as design features, and from them we learn geographical details in a pleasant manner—a suggestion offered in respectful humility to library boards and boards of education.

In the discussion of medical bookplates, attention was drawn to the fact that physicians use landscapes and mountains in their designs more extensively than do any other class. This observation must be extended to include librarians, for some of the most majestic and striking delineations of Californian scenery may be found in their plates.

In the bookplates of Lenala Martin, Jasmine Britton, and Josephine Whitbeck we note mountains *moderne,* snow crowned, or Alpine. Lenala Martin's mountain is the Matterhorn, as her maternal ancestors were born in Switzerland. The thistle is for her Scottish forbears, but the poppy reclaims her for California. Her plate was designed by Elsmore Lake.

The plate of Jasmine Britton with its Hokusai-print effect is beautifully individual. The silvery tone of the Japanese print was accomplished by Charles Joseph Rider, an artist active in the organization of the Bookplate Association International, as well as later an exhibitor and officer. Miss Britton's work for many years as head of the Children's Library is indicated in the lower left square, with its Greenaway children poring over a picture book. The majestic and untracked Sierra indicate both an interest and an affiliation, for the owner is a member of the Sierra Club. The chimney of her mountain cabin lifts a column of smoke, as

.(1 5 3).

if attempting to reach the peaks in the background. The plate is exquisite in its silvery tones, but the black and white rendition of the design is also arresting.

Josephine Whitbeck's plate by Franz Geritz indicates her interest in astronomy and nature in general. The late Ray Coyle did a Chaucerian plate for Alice Grover Whitbeck, in which familiar figures of the Prologue to

the *Canterbury Tales* are to be found. *Her Boke* completes the caption. The inn, troubadour, and streets are delightful as they surround the Nonne Preeste. Indeed, all that is missing is "the little man who seemeth busier than he was." The border of the plate tells the significant legend:

"But al that he mighte of his frendes hente,
On bokes and on lerninge he it spente."

Bertha Marshall's galleon puts in toward shore after sailing the Spanish Main. The armorial plate of Rebecca

Sharon MacNair is by James Cady Elwell. Verily the sum of human knowledge has been reduced through the skillful use of the pyramids in Miltona Thwing's bookplate by Donna Davis.

Leona Shepherd has designed for Helen Haines a bookplate brimful of personal associations. The motto, *With sail and oars,* is taken from the armorial bearings of the family coat of arms, as was also the bird on the swinging draperies. Beneath the trireme in the center is a row of books, but they are not the conventional volumes to be found in many bookplates. Instead, they are the bound volumes of the *Library Journal,* of which Miss Haines has been an editor.

A sculptural bookplate is always a pleasant variant from the usual, and Julia Bracken Wendt has designed a plate for Victoria Ellis in which the owner presumably has gone a-sailing in a perilous craft with a book for a sail. The only possible motto is that immortal line from Emily Dickinson which completes the border: *There is no frigate like a book.*

Muriel Alderman does not like to sew, and her plate confesses as much. The radio interests her more; also the children to whom as librarian she supplies books full of winged thoughts. The two elves in the border of the plate, designed by Margaret Ely Webb, suggest that in fairy-tale days a radio would have been magic.

Eleanor Homer, a well-known collector of bookplates, has a sepia-tinted engraving in which eucalyptus trees and mountains are the background for a group of books. Christine Price, who also collects bookplates, has a plate designed by J. Culbertson. The design shows Monterey Bay and the characteristic cypresses of that area.

Norah McNeill is another owner who chooses the eucalyptus as her favorite feature of the Californian scene, the fronded branches of the tree appearing in her design by Franz Geritz.

Among the bookplates of the librarians of the larger private libraries are the distinctive ex libris of Cora Sanders and the *Villa dei Sogni* plate of **Harrison Post**, both engraved by James Webb. Mr. Post's typographical plate is by John Henry Nash. Lucille Miller's typographical is by Ward Ritchie. Its sparing use of the Caslon flower indicates another of the myriad arrangements possible to this ornament, as well as the owner's typographical interests.

Elizabeth Brainerd Sawe has incorporated the Prometheus legend into a bookplate of significant Indian

symbolism. It is an imaginative representation of the fire bringer, a young Indian who persuaded Coyote, the familiar figure of Indian legend, to aid in bringing comfort and light; for primitive peoples in all parts

of the world have thought of a time when there was neither fire nor warmth nor light during darkness nor a
flame over which to cook food. This belief existed also
among Californian Indians, and through the cunning of
Coyote a coal of fire was stolen from the guardian spirits, the enemy of man. Henry Leonard Sawe has contrived
a plate of symbolism in characteristic locale, containing
desert shrub and cactus.

Nathan van Patten has a distinctive plate to mark
his books on Black literature. Jeannette Hitchcock's
linoleum cut by Marie McNutt indicates her profession,
which has lately led to ex libris writing.

Chapter XII

BOOKPLATES OF LOS ANGELES AND VICINITY

"August 1, 1769. Today I observed the latitude, and it came out for us thirty-four degrees and ten minutes north latitude.

August 2, 1769. . . We must have travelled about three leagues today. This plain where the river runs is very extensive. It has good land for planting all kinds of grain and seeds, and is the most suitable site of all that we have seen for a mission, for it has all the requisites for a large settlement." —Juan Crespí. *

THE bookplates of this "large settlement" are found to form an extensive group indeed, totalling over several hundred owned by residents who have builded this industrial empire. Since previous chapters have been devoted to the arts and professions, these geographical groupings will be found to comprise the industrial, commercial, mercantile, and generally useful members of society. The astute Crespí recorded as his observation a fact which twelve years later resulted in the founding of a city upon the site of the Indian village of Yang-Na. *El Pueblo de Nuestra Señora la Reina de los Angeles,* was founded on September 4, 1781, on the *Río Porciúncula,* by Governor Felipe de Neve, the second of the three pueblos to be established in Alta California.

.(1 5 9).

Other than the *marcas de fuego,* no Spanish bookplates have been found. But this occasions no surprise when one considers the conditions under which California was settled. In the early decades following the founding of the two larger cities, it would have seemed that the professional and military men among the scions of those endowed by the King might have brought from Spain and Mexico these attributes of a settled civilization. Ex libris records are found in many books in Mexico, for the first printing press in the New World was set up in Mexico City in 1539; and books and bookplates have been part of the culture of the sister republic from its earliest beginnings. Therefore aside from the books brought by the missionary fathers, for many years we have no record of privately owned or stray volumes; and histories regarding such books are perforce nonexistent.

The leather bookplate of the late William Andrews Clark Jr. and its armorial adaptation will be found in the magnificent volumes of his gift to the University of California. These mark but one of his benefactions, however, for this patron of the arts bountifully endowed the cultural life of his city. Engraved by Tiffany, this leather plate from the armorial combines the symbols of the owner's interests with the arms of Montana, the state of his birth.

Mrs. Edward L. Doheny has achieved in her design by Riviere and Sons of London one of the supremely beautiful leather ex libris known on several continents. The Edward L. Doheny Jr. Memorial Library at the University of Southern California possesses treasures of magnitude selected by this wise patron of the arts who has

.(1 6 0).

so fittingly marked them with a series of exquisite book-plates. The plate is an adaptation from a binding designed by Clovis Eve and found on a book entitled *Les Ordonnances de la Ville de Paris en 1582,* the center ornament of the binding being used. Engraved in gold upon the shades of leather which harmonize with the volumes they adorn, these tiny ex libris attain the chaste elegance of Georgian silver upon jewel tones of garnet, amber, ruby, and sapphire, eight shades in all. This plate is used in bibelot and folio in various sizes and is a tribute to all who have collaborated in its design. Mrs. Doheny also uses a typographical by Ward Ritchie, reminiscent of the Dove's Press compositions. There is a white leather plate for devotional and religious books, with the cross of the Equestrian Order of the Holy Sepulchre of Jerusalem, an order conferred upon the gracious owner.

The Harvey Seeley Mudd bookplate is also one connected with benefactions to education. It shows a Phoenician galley on the north coast of Cyprus; Greek columns and façade form the frame of the plate in which the coat of arms of the Street family is included, together with the insignia of the American Institute of Mining Engineers. The plate is the work of Bank Gordon and James Webb.

The name of George Allan Hancock is one which must be added to the artistic, scientific, and exploratory donations of citizens of Los Angeles. Rancho La Brea was a grant confirmed by Governor Echéandia and deeded to an ancestor of the present owner; from the ranch for many years an enormous quantity of asphalt, or *brea,* was extracted. It was in pits of this *brea* that prehistoric animals were caught, later to become a mine of scientific wealth and to form one of the most remarkable exhibits of its kind, the basis for the Hancock Room in the Los Angeles Museum. This plate represents the many scientific interests of the owner, as well as his musical, literary, and sporting avocations as witnessed by the minutely engraved navigator's certificate. The plate was designed by James Webb.

A few of the art treasures of the Willitts J. Hole collection are reproduced in infinite detail in a plate combining engraving and photogravure, wherein a Hopner, a Constable, a Ribera, and a Nicolas Poussin may be discerned. This plate was the work of James Webb. The plates designed by Sidney Armer for the Getz family have symbols of Californian significance, the Golden Gate plate for Milton and Estelle Getz being especially charming.

From the gold flakes of Marshall it is but a few decades to the *black gold* of our modern era. As an example of the industries depicted in bookplates, Louis Vail Cassaday's must lead all the rest. At first glance it might be a Japanese print, and the oil derricks, temples. Indeed the metaphor is not too far fetched, for the designer, Frances Cassaday Verbryck, describes the plate in terms not unlike our own: "The design is made for my brother's technical library and is the silhouette of his absorption plant on Signal Hill, with the wells in the background. If you are not familiar with such a plant, may I explain that it manufactures gasoline from the natural gas from the oil wells. The plants have the machinery housed in buildings with many windows which glow at night, and have a series of pipes outside which puff at the same time. The pagoda-like

structure in the rear is a cooling tower." Another ex libris with an oil-well derrick design is that of A. T. Jergins by Maxwell Hamilton Noll.

Rob Wagner's bookplate for Eleanor Banning recalls a name famous in the growth of the commonwealth, as General Phineas Banning is called the Father of Los

.(1 6 3).

Angeles Transportation. Famous also for the six-horse stage coaches, precursor of the stage lines to bear his name, General Banning is well known as the builder of the first local railroad.

Sadie and Sam Behrendt's plate is by Joseph Greenbaum and pictures the colonial doorway of the home once called the House of a Thousand Welcomes. Hillside, the Pasadena home of the late John Barnes Miller, is shown in his bookplate by Rob Wagner.

Frank, Mary, and Hugh Gibson's plate of triple ownership is replete with Californian associations, for each of these names has been of influence in the state. The plate was sent by the present Brazilian Ambassador and was the work of Carl Oscar Borg, who has caught much of the historical and personal with which the members of this gifted family are associated. The bar of music is the call of the Californian meadowlark and refers to the fact that Mrs. Frank Gibson brought before the legislature a bill to protect these birds.

A plate of considerable detail and sturdy balance is that of Lewis Webster Wickes, designed by James Webb for the mining and metallurgical engineer. In it a tramway with buckets is taking ore from the heights to the reduction works in the valley. The frame of the picture is a drift set from a mine tunnel with the vein and country rock depicted in a manner commonly used in mine maps. Certainly it is a plate pertaining to the owner alone, for the artist has added coat of arms, fraternal affiliations, insignia of two mining societies, and castle of the military engineering division. What appear, to the uninitated, to be astrological signs, are explained thus by the owner: "On the right of the

EX LIBRIS

FRANK
MARY
AND
HUGH
GIBSON

№

.(1 6 5).

upper ribbon in the circle is the ancient alchemist's symbol for the four metals: sun, gold; moon, silver; Venus, copper; and Saturn, lead.''

Elmer Gray's plate for his office library was designed by himself. Its classic columns bespeak the real architectural achievements, while the castle in the clouds indicates the future accomplishments. An unusual bookplate is that which John Barrow did for himself. It is reminiscent of his early days in frontier Montana, where he was familiar with Indian buffalo robes and their decorations. The running antelope is faithfully copied from an actual Indian robe.

The ship has ever been a favorite ex libris device and is a delightful symbol in the plates of the late Frank Hervey Pettingell, Helen Gladys Percey, Henry S. Clifford, Camilla S. Hellman, and Frederic Chandler Ripley. The plate of the latter is an etching by Franz Geritz, the unique design of clipper ship, lantern, and map describing the owner's avocation; the outspread log's nautical findings indicate his age, dwelling, and length of voyage. The motto further avers of the owner that *always a longing, a yearning uneasiness hasteth him on to the sea.* Max Wieczcorek must have imagined the Manila galleon itself when he created the bookplate for Andrew M. Chaffey.

The achievements of Dr. Ford Ashman Carpenter would be difficult to abridge in a single paragraph, but an editorial note makes mention of the following anomaly. He holds an international balloon pilot's license, is a lecturer at West Point Military Academy, was government consultant and meteorologist during the World War, and though he has flown practically every type of aircraft known, he has no knowledge of motor-car operation. His bookplate is the work of Charles H. Owens and Alexander W. Sharpe. It indicates, through the various types of balloons and aircraft, the owner's progress and identification with the science of aeronautics and its related subject, meteorology.

Al Keyrose and Marian Eells afforded their artists excellent canting devices, the latter plate being the work of Jerome Laudermilk. The plate of Clara Tester Stern is the third double-canting plate noted in this volume. The star is for the German surname, and *testa* is the Italian for *head*. Lyla and Maud Hawkins' hawk

.(1 6 7).

flies over the Mesa Verde cliff dwellings, the first of their kind to be discovered in the Southwest. The plate was designed by Charles Joseph Rider. It would be impossible to list all the canting designs on the bookplates of Californians. For those collectors who enjoy this variety, the canting plates of Phebe Estelle Spalding and Rose Margarethe Zobelein Lick may also be noted.

Book shops and browsers therein own many bookplates of which the Dellquest and Dawson plates are excellent examples of the ex libris art. The design of Carl Oscar Borg for the former is one in which armor and vessels of warrior vikings have been executed in painstaking detail. Ernest Dawson has two plates, one by Charles Joseph Rider and the other by Ruth Thomson Saunders. Family silhouettes, book shop, music, and the towering peaks of the Sierra are subjects common to both plates, but the contrasting methods of the two artists describe equally well the owner of the shop so widely known to Angeleños. Patricia Hunt states through her bookplate: *A jolly goode booke whereon to looke is better to me than golde.*

Jean and Jake Zeitlin use a typographical by Ward Ritchie, as also do Janet Hathaway Ritchie, Rosemary Heenan, and Wilbur Jordan Smith. Howard Moorepark's striking plate was designed by Paul Landacre. The woodblock of Lina Johnson, which pictures a grove of majestic trees, was designed by Foster Humphreyville. Cypress-fringed Monterey Bay is the subject of the woodcut of Barbara and Robert Niven, the work of Franz Geritz. The well-filled book shelves of the Arthur S. Bent library are depicted in his plate by Ralph Mocine, which is thought to date from 1895.

.(1 6 8).

The Homer of the "dear and dumpy twelves" and the epicure of roast pig live again in the bookplate of W. G. Farndale, an adaptation of one of Charles Brock's illustrations for Lamb's *Essays of Elia.* The owner describes it as picturing "Lamb in a characteristic fashion and surroundings outside an old London book shop, 'cheapening some old folio.' "

A bookplate of lyric beauty is that etched by J. W. Spenceley for Maud Teahon, La Rose 103. One possessing equal beauty and colorful associations is that designed by Harry French for the daughter of Lucky Baldwin. Rose trees, vines, shrubs, and a palatial dwelling appear in the background of the engraved plate of Anita Baldwin, while in the foreground prances a proud peacock. For Margaret Thompson of California, Ella Dwyer of Australia has etched an original plate in which the penguin book ends come to life at the sight of a well-loved book.

Other bibliophiles who use the armorial bookplate seem to have adopted the *armes parlantes,* the heraldic definition of the familiar canting plate wherein crest or motto is an adaptation or play upon the owner's name. Edward Alonzo and Clinton Talbot have a bookplate in which the *talbot,* or mastiff, forms the canting crest. Found in the volumes of Californian history and genealogical studies of the former, it is occasionally seen hand colored by Hattie Crippen Talbot.

A canting motto is noted in the Orra Eugene Monnette bookplate, which with its scarlet and azure tints is eminently fitted to mark the genealogical contributions and historical interests of the late publicist, writer, and banker. The Howland armorial was drawn by the late

.(1 6 9).

Major Charles Howland, another collector of Californiana. C. H. Cheney's oak tree suggests the *chene* of his
surname and towers above his coat of arms in the plate
designed by Sheldon Cheney. In Ella Fontenelle Tafe's
plate, the tree above the coat of arms indicates her interest

in genealogy, while the arms are those of the state seal of
Vermont.

Franz Mazareel's woodcut for Walter Otto Schneider
suggests a midnight plunderer of defenseless volumes.
Gaylord Beaman's plate, done by Paul Landacre, is a
view from his library.

The literary interests of James Strohn Copley are
blended with his out-of-door activities in a plate by

.(1 7 1).

Ben Kutcher, suggesting an ancient motto: *Mens sana in corpore sano.* The world of sports is indicated in the background of the mosaic-like detail. Gregg Layne's armorial has two Gaelic mottoes in it. The Heathcotes suggest pictorially their collecting specialties, as do Richard and Wayland Morrison, for whom Franz Geritz has designed plates showing their interest in American history and the history of chivalry.

Beautiful women, *mantillas,* roses, and *toreadores!* The following words taken from *Bolero,* an old Spanish folk song, might be an age-old scheme for romance:

Cuando en sus mantillas se pasean a la Alameda,
Allá vendrán bonitas con ros' y abanico;
Cuando la campanilla tocar a las ocho bonitas,
Danzar el bolero allá vendrán.

Together with the notes of the music, these lines may be read in a scroll flowing from a family coat of arms in the bookplate of Rose Margarethe Zobelein Lick. A member of the Alvarez family, she interprets her songs with hereditary skill; as a child she used to dance in the fiestas held at the old mission on the Plaza in Los Angeles. Thus enchanting memories are woven into the plate by Margaret Ely Webb, who has incorporated the apotheosis of California's beauteous background in a design of lace-like delicacy. The seated figure with fan and book is, in reality, a portrait of the owner's lovely daughter Rosemary, upon whom the *mantilla* rests with reposeful grace. Tiled patio, jasmine-vined trellis, plants in bright-hued pots, and the distant Sierra complete the plate in which may seen the *zobelein,* or little sable, appearing in the coat of arms. Another charming feature is the presence of plants representing

.(1 7 2).

Rose Margarethe Zobelein Lick

the flower names rose and marguerite which constitute it for ex librists a triple-canting plate. Rosemary Lick also has a bookplate by Margaret Ely Webb.

The *mañana* atmosphere of the Plaza is illustrated by Ralph Mocine in the plate of Clifford L. Graves, one of the earliest and indeed one of the few plates in Los Angeles to include the beloved landmark, the Plaza Church. The musical name of María Ernesta Ramona Lopez might be suggested by a mission bell in her plate which has been the inspiration of Rob Wagner. The bookplate by Henri de Kruif for Dolores Machado Barrow is another which possesses old Spanish family associations.

A favorite combination of artists is the heraldic-pictorial, as in Margaret McKenzie's plate, where the clan tartan and thistle have been designed, engraved, and hand colored by James Webb. The castle is that of the Earl of Seabright, the ancestral home. Book pile and library shelves often form an ideal accompaniment to the coat of arms, as in the James Long Wright and the Alma and Werner von Binzer plates. In several instances there are two or more coats of arms, as in Leota Woy's plate for Margaret Nye and in Maxwell Hamilton Noll's plate for himself, described in the Artists' chapter.

The Indian blanket from which the late A. C. Vroman evolved his exceptionally interesting bookplate is one of the large collection which is now distributed among the Metropolitan Museum, the Field Museum, and the Southwest Museum. Others of this group are illustrated in George Wharton James' long-out-of-print *Indian Blankets*. Although Mr. Vroman was recognized as one of Southern California's well-known bookmen, it is not so generally known that he was an authority on Indian

.(1 7 4).

matters and the owner of a valuable collection of objects relating to the subject. One regrets that the soft reds and grays of the Navajo design cannot be reproduced in the illustration of the plate. The central motif of Indian pic-

tographs encircles the name plate, and with swastikas completes an effective bookplate which was designed by W. C. Taverner in 1901.

Frederick Gray Jackson possesses an ex libris incorporating many ex libris associations, as well as

.(1 7 5).

showing collaboration with a master typographer of the modern era. When a bookplate is listed and authenticated by Charles Dexter Allen, it is news jubilantly shared, but when there are two such plates in one family, their combined stories are quite deserving of a few paragraphs of amplification. Part of this pleasant discovery has already been related in the section of Churches and Churchmen.

For the benefit of those readers who are unfamiliar with the ramifications of armorial ex libris classifications, it must be stated that these classifications coincide with several of the cabinet makers' periods: Chippendale, Jacobean, Rococo, Georgian, and other appellations conferred by various ex libris authorities such as Lord de Tabley, Walter Hamilton, or Egerton Castle. As in the case of furniture and architecture, it is sometimes impossible to draw date lines or to chart artistic divisions definitely.

Leaving such technicalities to the experts, we may consider that the Jackson plate, Allen 419, is an almost perfect example of a ribbon-and-wreath design by Nathaniel Hurd. With Henry Dawkins, Alexander Anderson, Joseph Callender, Peter Rushton Maverick, Paul Revere, and Amos Doolittle, Hurd ranks among the engravers and designers who constitute the Golden Age of American bookplate art. Many consider Hurd the most important of this group.

The adaptation from the original bookplate is illustrated here, bearing the signature of Bruce Rogers, an American typographer. The history of the plate, together with the trials undergone before the present owner, Frederick Gray Jackson, could actually insert it in his books, is a story which will be related entirely from his explanation, a kindness that has resulted in broadening the scope of this narrative to include influences of other cultures as they have been showered upon a cosmopolitan state:

N^o   [   ]

"The original bookplate was engraved by Nathaniel Hurd for my great-great-grandfather Jonathan Jackson, born in 1743, graduated from Harvard in 1761, and died in 1810. His mother was Dorothy Quincy, the famous Dorothy Q. . . Either my father or my grandfather had a rather unsatisfactory reproduction of the bookplate

.(1 7 7).

made with his name, Patrick Tracey Jackson, inserted. I was familiar with this plate from childhood. One day an uncle of mine produced an old dictionary bearing the only original Jonathan Jackson bookplate that I have ever seen. Signed N. Hurd, it had a yellow stain on one side. As I was interested in photography at that time, I took a dozen full-size photographs of this bookplate, trying various colored filters to take out the stain, putting my own calling card over the name, etc., all in the hope of being able to print my own bookplate photographically. Then I told Bruce Rogers about it, and he offered to take a try at it. He had a long search to find models for the *F* and *G,* until at last was found a type satisfactory to him. The signature relates the collaboration attendant upon the signature only, and does not refer to the coat of arms itself. You are welcome to make what use you can of my bookplate and its story, although I am not a bookplate collector and have only enough prints for my own use from the copper plate taken from the original."

Space permits but inadequate mention of the plates of Santa Barbara, one of the most historic sections of California. An entire volume should be devoted to the subject by some Barbareño ex librist who would write of its artists and owners and the fund of local color marking its bookplates. The writer presents this brief section in the hope that an opportunity will arise in the future to incorporate more details and information, missing at this writing.

Tierra Adorada was the *sobriquet* of Santa Barbara in the early days, for since its discovery in 1542 by Juan Rodríguez, better known as Cabrillo, it has been endowed with a distinguishing quality which is unique in a state of blessed cities. The jewel of the entire mission chain which was founded by the second *padre presidente,* Fermín Francisco Lasuén, it has been the Mecca of tourist pilgrims from all lands. Even commerce in this fiesta city is removed from mundane custom, for once a year upon the *Calle Estado* the daily routine is administered by citizen and official dressed in the costume of Spanish days for the duration of the festival. Indeed the fiesta atmosphere obtains throughout the year. One senses it in shops and studios such as the group known as *El Paseo de la Guerra,* which has been evolved from the home of *Comandante* Don José de la Guerra. The Hoffman plate reminds us that this plan was made possible by Bernard Hoffman, a civic figure who has served on various advisory and architectural boards of that city's reconstruction.

Philip Stanley Chancellor's bookplate was engraved by Ward Small and has this motto: *Laying off the harness of an overwearied thought and reposing in the beauties that another's brain has wrought.* The Blanche MacLeish Billings plate is the work of G. H. McCall, in which an intricate design symbolizing the arts and muses encloses a landscape.

The familiar view of Mission Santa Barbara from the garden side is shown in the Louise Esther Bates plate by Jessie B. Wallace. A different view of the mission tower is given in the bookplate of Bernard and Irene Hoffman, which has already been mentioned. From the hills above the mission, the view encompasses the elevation on which the mission stands, and includes the harbor in the distance.

Their Montecito home is pictured in the bookplate of George and Eleanor Coleman, wherein Monte Arroyo has been suggested by Cora J. Gordon. *Punta de los Cedros* is the subject of Ednah and Girvan Higginson's plate, which embraces mountains and sea in a characteristic

bit of the Channel country. It was engraved by Sylvain Guillot Gray of Paris.

Avis and Roger Boutell, of the Tecolote (Wise Owl) Book Shop in the Paseo de la Guerra, have a bookplate by Ward Small, containing a view of the Channel from their home. Max Fleischmann's yachting, sporting, and literary interests are portrayed in a plate engraved by A. N. Macdonald. This plate has been listed as follows: Carver 43; Fearing 92.

The Louise Hall Eddy plate by Margaret Ely Webb is a woodcut in peach and wood-brown. Miss Eddy's name has been transliterated into Chinese characters, which also make a sentence referring to the wild peach blossoms used in the design.

The story of the J. Kendall sketch book is one with so many Californian associations that it might have been placed in various sections of this volume; but as it is used by Mrs. Mark Lawrence Requa, the granddaughter now living in Santa Barbara, it is introduced in this section. Brimful of associations and points where its history touches our own, the original plate was described and its entertaining history related by the great-granddaughter, Amy Requa Russell.

J. Kendall was an Englishman who resided for a few years in New York, where he went after his marriage in England to the niece of Sir Joseph Paxton. Sir Joseph had been knighted by Queen Victoria for designing the Crystal Palace. Kendall, naturalized in his adopted country, contracted the gold fever and departed for San Francisco in 1849 on the bark *Canton*. It is thought that a company was formed in New York, in which all the passengers owned shares in the ship. The diary kept by Kendall on the long voyage around Cape Horn is to be published sometime in the future, but the sketch book had as frontispiece the design which is now used as a bookplate and which has never been altered to indicate present-day ownership. A record of naïve observations as to the flora and fauna of the

.(1 8 1).

new land, it contains exaggerations quite as delightful as the *Nuremberg Chronicle,* and fulfills all the qualifications for an excellent ex libris, if only the name of the owner were inserted.

The bookplate of Amy Requa Russell, as intricately detailed as a piece of *mille fleurs* tapestry, was designed by Katherine Barbour Leovy.

Chapter XIII

BOOKPLATES OF SAN FRANCISCO AND VICINITY

"I judged that if this site could be well popu-
lated as in Europe, there would be nothing finer in
the world, as it was in every way fitted for a most
beautiful city, one of equal advantages by land and
water, with that port so remarkable and capacious,
wherein could be built shipyards, quays, and whatever else might be desired."   —Pedro Font. *

THE story of Juan Bautista de Anza, who demonstrated that the overland journey from Sonora,
Mexico, to Monterey was possible, is the prelude to
the founding of San Francisco on September 18, 1776, the
establishment of pueblo and presidio and Mission Dolores, and the subsequent history of the city under
Spanish, Mexican, and American rule. This city is at once
the despair and the lodestone of writers, and needs only to
be mentioned to readers of a later day who will note
that among "equal advantages of land and water," the
bookplates of those living near the harbor of St. Francis are whatever might be desired.

Mention of San Francisco has been frequent in this
bookplate history, because of the fact that the first
known and dated modern bookplates were found in that
city, as well as those owned by pioneer bibliophiles

.(183).

and historic citizens. Other chapters perhaps begin with some Argonaut author or artist, attorney or physician, churchman or schoolman; therefore the description of these modern bookplates is but the natural progression of the Olds, Kirkham, and Haight plates.

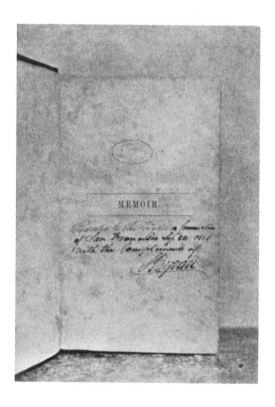

Proving the contention of the writer that for the special benefit of this volume art has most accommodatingly copied history, the hand-stamp of San Francisco's grimmest institution is here illustrated. It was while she was studying in the library of Robert E.

.(1 8 4).

Cowan and discussing the subject of early libraries with this man who has probably seen more of these books than has any other living Californian, that a tremendously important detail came up for discussion: the hand-stamp of the Vigilance Committee in a volume which was dated 1851.

Dutifully, if somewhat hastily, the writer recorded the fact, together with the signature of Stephen Payran, who had presented the volume to the Committee in 1851. Then this modern was gently detained, as the bibliographer said with Jovian calm: "But consider a little. This means that the Vigilantes meant to be a permanent institution. The very fact of literary possessions indicated their intention to remain organized, perhaps forever." Then he added, ruminating as one familiar with far-off things in an age removed from fledgling writers: "And have you ever heard for certain whether they did formally disband?" Not since the Phrygian liberty caps appeared on the bookplates of *citoyen* and *citoyenne* had such portentous associations emanated from a bookplate.

The hand-stamp was much in use in the early days, and numerous instances of these simple methods of indicating book ownership might be adduced. With the combination of the typographical and printer's label, the ex libris output in these pioneer localities could be expanded into a modest check list, but space does not permit. The admirable *Libraries of California,* by Flora Haines Apponyi, if it had resulted in any ex libris findings, would have been an interesting source book for ex librists. Several plates belonging to owners who are mentioned in it have been found; among them

.(1 8 5).

the canting plate of Henry P. Bowie is an engraved bookplate of interest. He was president of the Mercantile
Library Association and owner of a large library which
was described by Apponyi.

One of the most interesting of all the Californian
bookplates and also one of the earliest is the plate of
R. W. Kirkham, a lithograph in several slight variations.
An allegorical plate of considerable beauty but of more
historic interest, it is thought to be one of the first
representations of the Golden Gate. In it the typical
industries of the state—mining, commerce, shipping—
are indicated by the devices which surround the seated
figure of Agriculture. Sheldon Cheney suggested that
the plate might have been designed and executed by one
of the commercial engraving houses of San Francisco, of
which there were many and of which the output resembles
that of Currier and Ives for historical values. This
illustration was taken from one of the original plates
which, though mutilated, yet affords a clearer representation than a die from one less clear but in a complete state. Ralph Wilson Kirkham, who was a major
and quartermaster in the United States Army, came to
San Francisco in 1855. His very creditable library is

among those described by Apponyi in her *Libraries of California,* and grew to three thousand volumes before his death in 1893.

Harry Ellsworth Dore is a grandson of Benjamin

Dore, whose journal may be read in the publications of the Californian Historical Society. He has a plate designed by Beulah Mitchell Clute, in which is shown the two-dollar stamp of the Wells Fargo Pony Express.

The highest peak in continental United States appears on the bookplate of Josiah Dwight Whitney. In July, 1864, Mt. Whitney was named for the geologist who was then the head of the Geological Survey of California. The gently rolling Marysville buttes of historic Sutter County are shown in the background of the Ethel Swain plate, in the foreground of which W. J. Rice has added a delightful group of wild flowers.

.(1 8 7).

In a volume entitled *Rights and Duties of Merchant Seamen,* by George Ticknor Curtis, is an inscription by Edward Everett accompanying his armorial bookplate, Allen 263. The ship *Edward Everett* sailed from Boston with one hundred fifty passengers as owners and members of the Edward Everett California Mining and Trading Company. It left Boston on January 13, 1849, and arrived at San Francisco on July 7, 1849. A library of three

hundred volumes was presented to the company by the distinguished scholar and orator in whose honor it was named.

Another very early bookplate is that of Isaiah W. Lees. It is of the book-pile variety with two stars, one referring to his position as chief of detectives and the other to his office as chief of police. Two early armorial plates are those of George Frederic Parsons and Hall McAllister, brother of the famous Ward McAllister. Anson Parsons Hotaling's plate may be described as an armorial without benefit of the College of Heraldry. Together with the armorial design, the typographical label appears invariably in the early bookplate history of any locality. This is especially

.(1 8 8).

true of Mexico, where the typographical predominates; and in American ex libris history it antedates the armorial, for the earliest dated bookplates in the United States are of this variety. This fact may be verified by reference to Charles Dexter Allen. Among early Cali-

fornian typographicals are those of Joshua P. Havens of San Francisco, Harris Weinstock and Seth Babson of Sacramento. Mr. Babson, who arrived in California in April, 1850, after a trip around the Horn, became one of the state's earliest architects. He designed the homes of Leland Stanford and Charles Crocker, the Crocker Art

.(1 8 9).

Gallery, and other notable buildings. Also he worked on the early problem of flood control in Sacramento.

Against a background of a seventeenth-century map in which the *Californie Isle* is plainly seen, Dorothy Payne has etched a plate for John Howell containing his interests and specialties. The Bohemian Club might

also suggest his bookish interests as owner of the Shop of the Open Door. His famous collection of Bibles has been artistically and appropriately combined with his fraternal affiliations.

For the late Ellen B. Scripps, W. J. Fenn designed a bookplate in which a view of her home is the feature.

A plate which needs no explanation to the esoteric coterie of San Franciscans is that of Richard Sachse, in which the Ferry Building is glimpsed amid flying gulls. The name label might be enclosed by puffs of smoke trailing from the ferry boats, for the owner was interested in problems of transportation and was wont to do much of his reading while he was commuting from Berkeley. The plate was designed by W. F. Rauschnabel.

Native Californians who have indicated their individual interests in ex libris fashion are Joseph C. Winterburn and Charles Richard Sargent. Mr. Winterburn's paternal grandfather arrived in San Francisco in 1850 and became an honored name in the city of the Argonauts. A cartographer and an explorer, together with the Western hemisphere, appear in the plate designed by Phyllis

.(1 9 1).

Winterburn. Marcia Fee has designed the plate for Mr. Sargent in which his birthplace, Monterey, is delightfully indicated through the view of the bay and of the Monterey cypresses in the border of the design. The crossed rifles are for his rank as captain of infantry. A suggestion of his early life on a Californian ranch is also included.

Among public benefactors William Randolph Hearst has a bookplate which bespeaks wide associations and spheres of influence. William Wilke has achieved for Mr. Hearst a magnificent bookplate in which the classic symbolism indicates the interests of the journalist and publicist. In 1910 Carl Oscar Borg designed for Phoebe Apperson Hearst a bookplate which was engraved by Harry French. Mrs. Hearst owned another engraved plate which marked donations given by her to the University of California.

The plate of Marjorie and Martin Mitau transplants to book-loving San Francisco some of the magic of the book stalls along the Seine. As background, the towers of Notre Dame and the delicate spire of Sainte Chapelle complete an etching, by Paul Fleury, of misty beauty.

Many San Franciscans preserve their ancestral homes in design features of bookplates, using armorial bearings and individual symbols to personalize plates of modern ownership. In Myra Lumbard Palache's bookplate the lovely colonial home accompanies symbols of musical and literary interests. Maud Lee Flood's plate is of Linden Towers. Emma and Alfred Ehrmann's bookplate shows a home interior looking out on the Golden Gate. Alice and J. B. Levinson's music room also combines a view of the Golden Gate in the top panel of their plate, which was designed by William Wilke. Olive Holbrook Palmer writes that "five generations have enjoyed and visited in Elmwood, Menlo Park." The

plate, which was designed and engraved by Sidney Alabaster, pictures a few of the two hundred thirty elm trees which Charles Holbrook planted when he acquired the home in 1881. Coats of arms and Pekingese complete a pleasing plate.

From her home on storied Russian Hill, Helen M. Wells looks across San Francisco Bay to Mt. Tamalpais. A delightful memory of this view is perpetuated in a pencil sketch made by Frances Brooks, from which Miss Wells' bookplate was made. The home still standing on Russian Hill, pictured in the bookplate of Florence

Paul, was brought around the Horn in sections in the early pioneer days.

Florence Atherton Eyre's bookplate pictures "the historical house that was built in 1860, through whose ever-open door many distinguished people have passed. Unfortunately it is a thing of the past, having been destroyed by fire." Although Gertrude Atherton has no bookplate, it is a pleasure to include here a token of this famous old Californian family.

The Casa Alvarado in Coyoacán was engraved on wood by Howard McCormick for the bookplate of Zelia Nuttall. With a skill reminiscent of Timothy Cole, it is an admirable selection for the owner, who is an archaeologist. Miss Nuttall acquired this pictureque home of Juan Alvarado, a lieutenant of Cortés, the door of which is utilized as design feature completed by the starry constellation and shrine.

The founder of the Order of Friars Minor would have loved the legend of the swallows of Mission San Juan Capistrano. In truth, it is no legend, for each year on

Casa
Alvarado

Zelia Nuttall

.(1 9 5).

March 19, the feast of St. Joseph, there has arrived, according to the mission records for sixty-eight years, a cloud of birds to nest in the eaves of the historic mission. The bookplate of Harry Bennett Abdy pictures this mission in a design by Rowena Meeks Abdy. On the plate of Thomas Wayne Norris, Mission Carmel is shown

in its pre-restoration state. The well-known Mission Dolores in San Francisco appears on the bookplate of Mary Louise Phelan, designed by Pedro Joseph de Lemos. This completes a trio of plates which contain sketches of actual missions.

B. J. S. Cahill ingeniously includes in his bookplate a plan of the Civic Center, which has been his life

.(1 9 7).

work. The series of maps represents his labors in perfecting a world map which he has called *la mappemonde de l'avenir*. The framework of the design suggests the owner's profession, architecture, and the urns refer to the fact that he has designed two of the largest columbaria of the world.

The plate of the distinguished senator, James Duval Phelan, has been assigned to an earlier chapter; yet it possesses a deep significance as the symbol of San Francisco. It was sent through the courtesy of Noel Sullivan, who expresses his regrets that copies of this rare plate are not available.

Richard Montgomery Tobin has a bookplate of musical associations, for the scroll includes the opening notes of the *Passion of St. Matthew,* by Bach. Of this plate Mr. Tobin writes: "Designed by Koninenberg, the eminent Dutch painter, its symbolism refers to my six years in Holland as United States Minister. The tulip is the national flower, and the scroll and the violin refer to the musical character of the country and the splendid production of Bach's masterpiece which takes place every year in Amsterdam. The fawn and the lark typify fidelity."

Of similar origin is the plate of Prentiss N. Gray. The work of A. van Neste, it was designed in appreciation of Mr. Gray's services on the World War Food Commission. Against a background of the city of Antwerp is a barge bringing food to the Belgians.

The plate of one of California's most distinguished servants is that of Herbert Hoover, in which the design possesses a great deal of interest for the layman as well as those familiar with mining topics. The central

EXLIBRIS
RICHARD·MONTGOMERY
TOBIN

portion is a reproduction of an old woodcut in a very early book on mining published in 1527 under the title *Ein Nutzliches Bergbüchlein von Allen Metallen.* The Latin version of this book is more familiar to those who know of the technically difficult feat of translation made by Herbert Hoover and Lou Henry Hoover of

De Re Metallica, by Georgius Agricola, a German miner whose baptismal name was Georg Bauer. This translation appeared in 1912, the edition closely approximating the original. Of it Mr. Hoover once said: "The book is a milestone on the road of civilization, for except the book of Genesis the only attempts to explain natural phenomena had been those of the Greek philosophers and

.(2 0 0).

alchemists." Mr. Quinan adapted the bookplate as described above and also added figures which complete symbols of mining significance. The plate was designed especially for the extensive Hoover collection of old mining books.

Other bookplates in which the symbols of mining and engineering significance are noted are those which were designed by Donna Davis for Robert Wallace Pack and Edward Morris.

Modern devotees of the typographical are James K. Moffitt, H. L. Tevis, Mrs. Clinton B. Hale, and William Clarkson Van Antwerp. James K. Moffitt has another bookplate, an engraving by Stern of Paris, which suggests his classical interests. The minute typographical of Templeton Crocker is used to mark his collecting specialties.

The first monument of any kind to be dedicated to Robert Louis Stevenson was erected in Portsmouth Square, the landmark usually designated as the Plaza. It was the thought of a number of San Francisco citizens and friends of "the strange-looking shabby shack of a fellow" who dwelt in the city, that they might be included in the immortality destined to be his. Although he was ill and despondent during much of his stay in San Francisco, his genius was early recognized there, and his allusion to that city in the sketch, *A Modern Cosmopolis,* was to become more prophetic than he realized at the time:

"The mere extent of a man's travels has in it something consolatory. That he should have left friends and enemies in many different quarters gives a sort of earthly dignity to his existence; and I think the

.(2 0 1).

better of myself for the belief that I have left some in California interested in me and my success."

The combined efforts of Willis Polk, Bruce Porter,

and George Piper evolved the fountain and monument topped by the *Hispaniola* on a granite shaft upon which was inscribed an excerpt from *A Christmas Sermon.* The monument was unveiled on October 7, 1897, eight years before the St. Gaudens statue was erected in Edinburgh. In Donna Davis' design for the bookplate of the late Dorothea Melinda Melden, it was fitting that the subject chosen was the owner's favorite author.

A chance remark supplied several clues that plates of early pioneers might be found in Stockton. Through the kindness of Harry Noyes Pratt several were located, alas, to be described in detail in a later volume. But the armorial of the self-styled Lord Lewis Chalmers, a wealthy Britisher who poured out quantities of British gold in an attempt to bring forth a rival to the Comstock Lode, offers another temptation to digress with tales of owners whose lives enter unexpectedly into this narrative. There is an armorial bookplate belonging to Louis Terah Haggin, to whom a memorial gallery has been erected in Stockton.

Chapter XIV

BOOKPLATES OF SCHOOLS AND SCHOOLMEN

"Where marshes teem with death shall meads unfold,
Untrodden cliffs resign their stores of gold;
Where slept perennial night shall science rise,
And new-born Oxfords cheer the evening skies."
—Timothy Dwight. *

WHEN the president of Yale College wrote the above lines in 1794, he might have been describing the educational development of the Pacific coast. Seldom has a locality been blessed with such a variety of institutions of higher learning as has California. Laurance Hill in *Six Collegiate Decades* characterizes the prophecy prefigured by Timothy Dwight as "perhaps the most remarkable growth of colleges and universities in a given area during a given time in all history."

Carrying on the tradition of culture present at the very inception of the state, this fabric of education has been the foundation of progress through which have been unfolded pueblo and village, trading post and city. Though this subject has contributed to other chapters, the entire field presents a distinguished array, for the schools and colleges of California have contributed to the art of ex libris as specifically as they have to the muses whose combined academic inheritance they have so liberally dispensed.

.(2 0 4).

The official seal of the University of Southern California contains a tiny view of Old College, the oldest building on the campus, of which the cornerstone was laid in 1884. The institution, however, was actually founded in 1880, on September 4, the ninety-ninth anni-

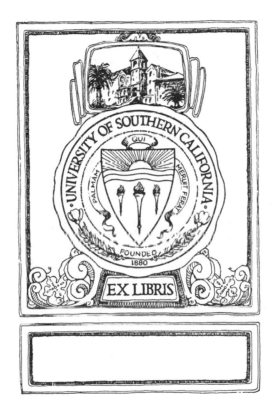

versary of the founding of the city of Los Angeles. This great university was made possible by the gift of land of Ozro Childs, former Governor J. G. Downey, and Isaias Hellman, but it was the thought of a group of public-spirited men of the then growing city.

.(2 0 5).

The bookplate of the Seeley Greenleaf Mudd Gift to the Hoose Library of Philosophy uses heraldic mantling, together with the wheel for the Mudd family's interest in engineering and the *fleur de lis* for their French ancestry. The helmeted Trojan reminds us of the cognomen of these later-day students who "lift Trojan glory

to the skies," in a prowess known throughout the land.

This university owns a number of excellent plates to mark benefactions, memorials, and bequests, and to constitute a reminder of former students and professors who have taken part in its intellectual history. There is a bookplate for the Los Angeles University of International Relations, which recalls the special interest

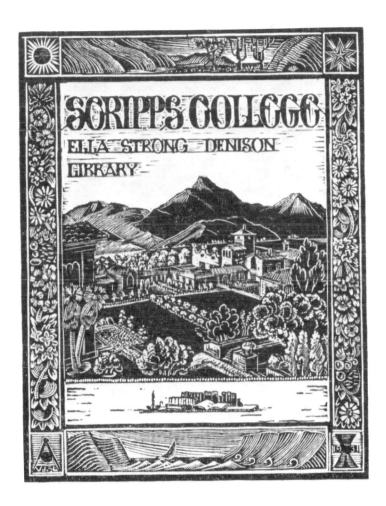

SCRIPPS COLLEGE
ELLA STRONG DENISON
LIBRARY

.(2 0 7).

of the distinguished president, Rufus B. von KleinSmid.

Claremont, Scripps, and Pomona Colleges comprise the group called the Oxford of America. For Pomona College Ruth Thomson Saunders has designed the Harwood Court plate. Scripps College uses a plate which is

almost a miniature guide to the campus, for in it may be located the Ella Strong Denison Library, Eleanor Joy Toll Hall, Ellen Browning Hall, and Susan Miller Dorsey Hall. This plate, which is used for the library, was designed by the late Virginia Litchfield Clark. In the border is a panorama of typical Californian scenery, showing sea, mountain, and desert, interwoven with flowers and fruit of the state. Claremont College uses plates in

.(2 0 8).

CHARLES H. PRISK
LIBRARY
OF
ENGLISH
LITERATVRE

OCCIDENTAL
COLLEGE
LOS ANGELES
CALIFORNIA

.(2 0 9).

which the college seal accompanies panels indicating the various bequests.

In the opinion of many, Robert Louis Stevenson is the dean of English Literature. A characteristic portrait of him has been sketched in the plate of the Charles H. Prisk Collection for Occidental College. The printing press represents the donor's profession, journalism. The plate was the work of Charles Joseph Rider. The Occidental College Chapter of Phi Gamma Delta has a typographical design by Ward Ritchie.

The Spanish language has lent grace to these pages through phrase and proverb, sometimes through translation of place names of past or present history, but the motto on the bookplate of the Southwest Museum is of more than passing beauty: *Mañana flor de sus ayeres.* In fact, these words might characterize the Spanish heritage in California, for its prophecy is couched in poetic thought: *Tomorrow shall be the flower of their yesterdays.*

The seal announces that the Museum was incorporated in 1907. The Aztec symbol is the serpent of wisdom combined with the eagle of vision and power. The names of Adna R. Chaffee, Norman Bridge, Frederick Webb Hodge, James A. B. Scherer, Hector Alliot, J. S. Torrance, and M. R. Harrington are connected with its establishment, endowment, and growth. The plate for the Munk Library of Arizoniana was designed by Hernando G. Villa, with Charles Francis Lummis posing as the model for the Indian.

A delightful view of San Francisco Bay may be seen beyond the wrought-iron gates of Ethel Moore Hall of Mills College, in the pictorial bookplate designed by

LIBRARY

OF THE

SOUTHWEST
MUSEUM

William Wilke. Its inclusion here will be the source of pleasant memory to former students, for the scene is the open-air fireplace, the meeting place for festivity as well as study.

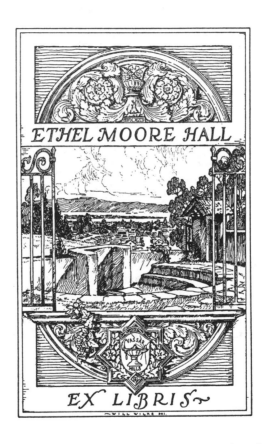

The peak viewed from a library interior in the Norman Delarue Cox Memorial bookplate is Mt. Diablo. The plate, Andreini 209, was engraved by J. W. Spenceley for St. Matthew's School in Burlingame, which school also has an earlier plate by Haig Patigian. This school was founded by the father of the Reverend William A. Brewer, whose name has appeared so often in these pages. It was while he was assistant in this institution that he began his famous collection of ex libris.

Majestic San Francisco College for Women has a bookplate which was designed by its architect, H. F. Minton. The giant cross on Lone Mountain has been a landmark since 1862, when it was erected by Archbishop Joseph Sadoc Alemany. History relating to this cross and to the purchase of the land surrounding it is part of the annals of San Francisco. The plate of Monsignor Joseph Gleason mentioned in an earlier chapter reminds us of his magnificent gift of a collection of incunabula to this institution. Of the Lone Mountain cross he wrote:

"In all the hectic history of these sixty-seven years it has looked down upon the progress of the metropolis as it developed through trial and travail to conquest and achievement. Gambling manias, riots, upheavals, money madness, the rise and fall of the great and near great in citizenry, preparations for wars, fires, earthquakes, utter devastation, and hopeful reconstruction, the old cross on Lone Mountain has seen them all, 'serene, indifferent of fate.' "

The earliest plate of the Dominican College of San Rafael was one by W. K. Briggs, which contained a view of the imposing façade of this college. The newer plate shows an exquisite reproduction of Fra Angelico's *St. Dominic,* together with the seal of the order forming the staff of the institution.

Completing the group of colleges in Northern California are two very early typographical plates: one of them, that of Santa Clara College, being the earliest dated plate in this group, July, 1858; and the other, that of the old California College at Vacaville.

A number of high schools own bookplates, many of them the result of competitions instituted by their art departments. Among these are the John Burroughs, Le

Conte, and Mt. Vernon Junior High Schools of Los Angeles. Banner Peak and Mt. Ritter top the plate of the John Muir School in Berkeley. A *Sequoia gigantea,* a Douglas fir, a friendly chipmunk, and a squirrel complete this pleasing plate by Beulah Mitchell Clute.

A history of the plates of educators of California,

EX·LIBRIS
JOHN·MVIR·SCHOOL
BERKELEY·CALIFORNIA

.(2 1 5).

added to that of the institutions which they have ruled, would be transactions to be written into the history of education in the United States. This is particularly true of the leaders of universities, for such men as a Jordan or a Wheeler, a Barrows or a Wilbur have filled those offices, even deserting them temporarily to lend talents to international committees, cabinets, letters,

Library of

Benjamin Ide Wheeler

and politics. It would be impossible to chart the full line of their endeavors, but a study of their bookplates and the personal symbolism involved will often betray hints of usefulness undertaken for humanity, and will remind us of achievements which have carried their owners far beyond college halls and the more tranquil academic labors.

Benjamin Ide Wheeler's *discobolus* plate is engraved with intaglio clearness enshrining the classic figure within a cameo setting. Robert Gordon Sproul's bookplate resembles an incunabulum illustration, for in it legendary gryphons support a shield with his initials beneath a tree sheltering leering Gothic creatures. It is, however, an adaptation from the printer's mark of Philippe Pigouchet, a fifteenth-century printer.

In Beulah Mitchell Clute's designs for schoolmen, an incredible amount of detail is employed within a pleasing composition. Her bookplate for Edward Oliver Essig of Berkeley indicates several achievements of the

.(2 1 6).

owner, whose chief interest is entomology undertaken for its benefit to Californian industries. The Easter Morn iris is his creation; the fuchsia another of his horticultural specialties. A decoration from the French government is glimpsed; also his fraternal and educational interests, together with the nature research which occupies part of his leisure time. The Campanile is seen in his bookplate as well as in the design of Charles Atwood Kofoid, whose plate has much of personal symbolism ranging from *objets d'art* which were the gifts of rulers and potentates in a life brimful of academic adventure, to the fifty-seven (by actual count) varieties of bacteria which he has met in his exploratory and marine studies.

The director of the California Institute of Technology might be expected to own a bookplate with a design of electrons flanked by abstruse mathematical theorems, but his plate is one in which the university towers of a campus are glimpsed through the leaded windows of his library. It was designed by Harry Leslie Walker, and is the joint plate of Robert and Greta Millikan.

The president of Stanford University, Ray Lyman Wilbur, indicates by a medallion in the lower right corner of his bookplate that he was once the chief of the Conservation Division of the Food Administration. The view of the rolling hills is that seen from his library, and the design is the work of Alice Kimball.

James Main Dixon's plate is full of interest as a history of mediaeval colleges, and in it we learn some-

thing of the history of ancient St. Andrews University in Scotland. Born in Burns' town of Auld Ayr, he attended Edinburgh University and served for a time on its faculty before going in the same capacity to St. Andrews. The scholar's hat on the plate is the same as that used in the University of Paris, the mother of the Scottish institution. "French influence was dominant in the Scotland of the fifteenth century," writes this professor of English Literature at the University of Southern California, "the alliance being a close one, and a Scot being the only foreigner then admitted to

.(2 1 8).

the rights of French citizenship.'' The plate was the
design of Charles Joseph Rider, who has suggested the
owner's ancestry by the heraldic figure of his coat of
arms and the thistle.

Willis Linn Jepson, botanist and authority on Californian *silvae,* owns one of the most historic plates

SOMETHING · LOST · BEHIND · THE · RANGES · OVER
YONDER · · GO · YOU · THERE · · the explorer

WILLIS LINN JEPSON

in the state. Its covered wagon pushes on through the
desert wastes to the promised land, its motto voicing
the lure of the unknown. The plate was designed by
Helen M. Gilkey.

The charming plate of the Shakespearean scholar,
Fredric Mason Blanchard, weaves the eglantine and the

cowslip with the ceremonial of all lovers of garden and library. The Armin Otto Leuschner plate completes a group of designs made by Beulah Mitchell Clute for faculty members of the University of California. In this bookplate design the head of the Department of Astronomy pictures for us the first telescope invented by Galileo.

EX LIBRIS
AURELIA HENRY REINHARDT

I saw that in its depth far down is lying
Bound up by love together in one volume,
What through the universe in leaves is scattered.
PARADISE XXXIII, 85-87.

The president of Mills College, Aurelia Henry Reinhardt, is known to be a thorough student of Dante. For her bookplate William Wilke evolved a silhouette of the Florentine, and John Henry Nash was responsible for the typography. Ralph Tyler Flewelling of the Department of Philosophy of the University of Southern California uses a motto in his bookplate which is applicable to nautical discoveries or philosophical adventures: *'Tis not too late to seek a newer world.* The ship, bearing upon its sail the lion of his coat of arms, was designed by Geraldine Carr.

The arcade of the Santa Barbara State Teachers College is shown in the plate of the late Frank H. Ball, once president of the institution. Anna Head's plate is an armorial. Margaret S. Carhart's plate contains a

.(2 2 0).

delightful view of her home, and James McBurney has added a spray of marguerites for a canting device.

Dr. Max Farrand, director of research at Henry E. Huntington Library, owns a plate made by the Merrymount Press to mark his collection of the books of that press. This collection is to be given to the Huntington Library. Beatrix Farrand's bookplate is also a typographical label within a border of massive oak trees.

Chapter XV

BOOKPLATES OF STAGE AND SCREEN

"One man in his time plays many parts."
—William Shakespeare. *

THROUGHOUT this chapter the terms motion picture and theater will be used interchangeably, a feat which might not have been accomplished before the invention of sound recording and which is here noted to imply a fact of contemporaneity more than to suggest that the arts themselves are devoid of differences.

Cinema history records that the first film in this locality was shot in Los Angeles on May 3, 1904. It was what might be termed today a short subject, of Roy Knabenshue's pioneer dirigible balloon. However, production for commercial purposes was not started until Francis Boggs and Thomas Persons began work on *Across the Divide* on February 4, 1908. This is the date which actually initiated the motion-picture industry as we know it today.

At that time Hollywood was a pleasant village made notable through the exquisite floral paintings of Paul de Longpré, painter, botanist, and gentleman of France. From then until the present, its history has been world property; its entertainment efforts have become the visual *esperanto* of the twentieth century. The lives, rôles, yes, and the bookplates of the American cinema

.(2 2 2).

possess a glamor for the rest of the world; for these decorative people live exciting, yet thoughtful lives as we learn by studying their hobbies and collections.

Incidentally their bookplates have been difficult to procure, for evidently the most efficient secretary is she who brings the least to the master's attention. Glittering photographs often came as the result of a request for plates; or, again, these elusive people change their addresses quite as often as their rôles and costumes. Yet the proverbial camaraderie of a fascinating profession is theirs; interviews and contacts are checkered with tales of research and of book hunts for illustrations; of treks from continent to continent for authentication of locale; of first editions, points, and issues. Young interviewer, arm yourself with technical questions regarding hobbies and collections, for the world is the oyster of these devotees of the mask and buskin. Therefore it is with considerable pride that I am able to present—to adopt the phraseology of the theater—these ladies and gentlemen of the Silver Sheet in the Golden State.

Perhaps the plate in the industry which carries with it the earliest historic associations is that used by Tom Miranda. The present adaptation was made by Greta Garde from the seal used in the state papers of his illustrious great-great-grandfather, Francisco de Miranda. Of the founder of the Venezuelan Republic, Herbert E. Bolton has this to say: "Washington and his associates merely started the American Revolution. Miranda, Bolívar, San Martín, Hidalgo, Morelos, and Iturbide carried it through." Truly this bookplate is one which hies us to our history books, for our sister republics to the south have played a notable part in the annals of our state.

There is a bookplate designed by E. M. Bendowna and

bearing the name Helena Modrzehewska Chalapowska. The distinguished Polish tragedienne who was better known as Helena Modjeska visited our shores several decades ago and remained to live in her Forest of Arden home in Southern California. The sylvan beauty of the design of the bookplate is enclosed within a Greek column upon the pediment of which is reproduced her coat of arms.

The first house built in La Jolla was that called The Green Dragon by one of Southern California's most picturesque living characters, Anna Held. This delightful cosmopolitan is the Anna Held of Berlin (not Paris), who as a young woman was a close friend of Ellen Terry and Henry Irving. After brilliant years in England she came to San Diego, and later designed and built her story-book houses all over her La Jolla hill. At that time local architecture was of the Eastlake period, or Californian Perpendicular, which has been defined by Olive Percival as having "bay window and side porch, with wooden lace trim." To the La Jolla homes of today,  constituting the atmosphere with which we moderns associate the village which the Spanish named *The Jewel,* Miss Held gave attractive names, alluring fireplaces, and latticed casement windows that looked upon the blue Pacific. According to Olive Percival, who visited often at The Green Dragon, Miss Held's home was a lodestone for artists, musicians, writers—for those whom the younger Californians will probably always designate as the Modjeska coterie. Ellen Terry, of course, came. The bookplate was the gift of Gordon Craig, who sent it from England for use in the volumes of The Green Dragon home. The house received its name from one of the novels of the owner's friend, Beatrice Harraden. Anna Held later became the wife of Max Heinrich, the great *lieder* singer, whose story should be related in connection with Californian musical history.

I am grateful, first, to the gracious owner and, next, to Olive Percival, the recipient of the Craig block, for their share in contributing this memento of dramatic history of the nineties.

Immortality might be demonstrated by the effect which Rudolph Valentino's ex libris seems to have upon those viewing his plate designed by William Cameron Menzies. The spirited battle scene between Saracen and Crusader illustrates a fact not generally known; for the chivalric owner was a collector of old armor and firearms, and his collection constituted a valuable reference library of warfare in all ages. Shield, armor, trappings, and flash of spear and lance are drawn with careful attention to chronology and detail.

Another memory evoked of the early days of the industry is the bookplate of the late June Mathis, which is fittingly mentioned at this juncture, for she it was who wrote the script for *Four Horsemen of the Apocalypse,* one of the brilliant efforts of Valentino. Her bookplate is one of the few to utilize the motion-picture camera.

Emil Ludwig has said that "the history of our time must devote special attention to the unparalleled world success of Charles Chaplin because he reveals the

Ex Libris
Rudolph Valentino

.(2 2 7).

profound longing of the age.'' The universal coinage of comedy is founded upon the props of the bookplate which is illustrated here. The hat, shoes, cane, and moustache were grouped by the studio photographer at the suggestion of Mr. Reeves, the comedian's general manager. Surely this is fame of a very high degree, for even Kings and Queens must sign their Christian names.

Rob Wagner has designed for the inimitable Charlot another plate in which the sun, hidden beneath an enormous mask of comedy, shines upon the distant tower of the Houses of Parliament and the dome of St. Paul's. From the slums of Lambeth a ragged urchin looks across at all this vested splendor, in his right hand leading a dog and in his left bearing a wreath of laurel. A macabre note is struck by the dead bodies in the foreground, for it is over the wrecks and disappointments of others that Fame seems to beckon to the youth who was ultimately to become better known throughout the world than his own King.

John Barrymore's bookplate was designed by himself and uses the more familiar masks of comedy and tragedy, with a newer symbolism. The barren tree encircles the mask of tragedy, while the fruitful tree bears the mask of comedy. The crossed pens illustrate the versatility to be expected from any member of this royal family.

The delicate laciness of an old valentine has been executed by Ruth Thomson Saunders in this wood engraving for May Robson. In a design of deftness and charm, a tactful suggestion of stardom is made in an original manner. An inscrutable Pekingese ignores with celestial disdain a canary whose luxurious cage forms an artistic balance to three theatrical masks, for Miss Robson is fond of both dogs and birds. From the right of  the design extends a hand, holding an old-fashioned bouquet to suggest the applause of an audience for this perennial favorite of stage and screen.

George Hopkins' plate was designed by himself and suggests the kingship of cats by the regally jewelled Persian. The plates of Ben Alexander, Joel Swenson, and the late Theodore Roberts use the ship as an ever decorative symbol of romance as derived from books. Ben Kutcher's design for Ben Alexander is as intricate as tapestry, through a frame of which one glimpses an impossible hill of glass far away in a perilous sea. Waving pennons, a fearsome figurehead, and embroidered

.(2 2 9).

sails adorn the ship which is returning to the castle, bearing a prince who longs for more worlds to conquer. In William Powell's plate the turning leaves of a book release a dream castle of turrets and towers piercing the sky.

Jeffrey Mayer Selznick's Jabberwock plate is none other than a princeling sea horse, as is proved by the swishing tail and twirling fin and head surmounted by a silver crown. The plate, which was designed by Hugo Rumbold and engraved by James Webb, enjoys the distinction of being the youngest ex libris in the volume. This adorable plate is developed in nautical blue with silver and black. The signature must not be overlooked, for the youthful scion of the screen has signed it with a scrawl displaying the unmistakable illegibility of genius.

Herbert Brenon's bookplate contains objects of classic significance as well as personal symbolism, the main figures representing John Gutenberg and William Shakespeare. The plate was designed by William Wilke and printed by John Henry Nash.

Jean Hersholt is a Thespian whose proper classification here has caused difficult editorial problems. Perhaps he should have been placed in the Artists' chapter, for he has designed his own plate which possesses a world of personal significance. The Danish flag for the land of his birth and the flag of his adopted country are crossed beneath a mask which is not the conventional, but a copy of the oldest Greek mask in existence. Burning tripods suggest the adoration of the Greeks for arts and sports. As Mr. Hersholt pointed out, "the arts were as integral a part of the Olympic Games as were sports, and burning tripods were given as prizes in the Olympic Games.'' The rose is his favorite flower, and the palette is the sign of his avocation.

Alfred Santell and Malcolm Stuart Boylan use non-pictorial plates which leave nothing to the borrower's

imagination. The bookplate of the former is graced with beautiful lettering, clothing a gentle exhortation to return the volume to its waiting fellows. But the book-plate of the latter softens his no less definite state-ment by saying: *It is even more important that this volume be read than that it be returned promptly,* a variant of the saying of the immortal Jean Grolier, which has been such a legend throughout bookplate history: *Jo. Grolierii et amicorum.*

Egyptology has long been an absorbing topic for Fred Niblo, as is indicated in the design by William Spencer Wright. The incredible industry of Howard Greer is in no wise indicated in the plate drawn by this famous costumer of the stars, for his bookplate pictures a lazy young man in a hammock.

Hetty Gray Baker is welcome in a Californian book because she aids in the destinies of a major film corporation in New York; because she has written what is thought to be the first essay on bookplates of motion-picture actors; and because she has been exposed to Californiacs all her life. She writes: "My grandfather and several of my grandmother's uncles went out during '50 and '51 . . . to say nothing of my having been taught by my father that California was the greatest of states and San Francisco was the most alluring of cities." Her Stanley Harrod bookplate was suggested by William Fox's screen title for *This Freedom,* and she herself devised this ingenious way of announcing book ownership.

The writer intrudes at this juncture to opine that if she had begun a drive for quadruple-canting plates, it might not have proved *introuvable,* for three double-canting plates have already been discovered in her ex libris travels, as well as one triple-canting plate. Hetty Gray Baker's buxom cook is also reproduced on gray paper, thus becoming a collectible specialty. Perhaps this plate is the reason why Miss Baker collects and writes about canting plates. Following the theme of Miss Baker's *This Freedom* plate, a number of others form a classification which she calls histrionic plates. Several actors and actresses have utilized stills or allusions to their favorite rôles, certainly a pleasant manner in which to imprison early footlight memories. William Farnum has a still of himself as Sydney Carton in *The Tale of Two Cities*. Neil Hamilton's first great

rôle was in the Griffith production *America*. On the bookplate of Elsa and Neil Hamilton is his name suggested in electric lights by the artist, Richard Ewing. Perhaps this group should also include the hat-and-shoe plate of Charles Chaplin.

The brilliant red and gold of Cecil B. De Mille's bookplate provide an instantly recognizable label, the phoenix myth being its inspiration. Bebe Daniels owns a leather ex libris tooled in gold by James Webb. The same artist has engraved a plate for Roderick La Rocque. Irving Cummings uses a tiny plate with an intaglio-like Greek head. Minna Gombel's is an armorial in a *moderne* adaptation. Mell Efird's bookplate might be the ideal of anyone who appears before the footlights, for her woodcut by Paul Landacre has evoked the witchery and glamor of the theater.

The plates of Hobart Van Zandt Bosworth and the late John Gilbert show library interiors. For the latter, Leota Woy's design features an exquisitely paned window before which is an old silver lamp once used in a cathedral in Mexico. *My library was dukedom large enough,* announces Mr. Bosworth, whose plate boasts a mediaeval scholar and navigation instruments for the owner's collection of books pertaining to nautical subjects.

Dugald Stewart Walker wrought for Reginald Barker a veritable magic wand, as his bookplate evokes the presence of the theater in employing many of the implements of romance and "faery lands forlorn." The velvet curtains are drawn aside to reveal a grove of *Midsummer Night's Dream* beauty into which the lovers retreat. Moth and Peaseblossom might be the fairy musicians in the corners, while peacocks and exotic plants add their notes of beauty to this enchanted forest. Scarcely a more severe contrast could be suggested than the typographicals designed by Ward Ritchie for Lynn Riggs and Gloria Stuart; yet these plates lose nothing in fitness through comparison with their pictorial fellows.

Edward Everett Horton's bookplate demonstrates his fondness and respect for trees. He told Ben Kutcher during the designing of this plate that he used to

EX LIBRIS

MEL EFIRD

.(2 3 5).

declaim in forests. Hence it is no wonder that the tiny figure in doublet and hose is gracefully bowing, as he sweeps cloak and feather-crowned hat to the greensward. Two masks of comedy adorn this bookplate, for the in-

imitable actor has naught to do with tragedy.

Granting that the motion-picture industry in itself constitutes one of California's unique characteristics, we must consider Richard Wallace's bookplate a miniature Californian seal. Here the flag of the bear, a vignette from the actual seal, characteristic landscape, and the Golden Gate are combined with a film strip and its newest accompaniment, the sound track. Typical of Mr. Wallace's director-activities, the plate enables the un-

initiated to view the celluloid indications of the device which has constituted another epoch in the history of the film. It was drawn by Leota Woy, who was also the designer of the bookplates of Jason Shepherd Joy and Frank Anthony Fay.

For Gabriel S. Yorke's plate, Kenneth Fagg worked out a design containing the owner's philosophy of life and indicating some of his travels. On a visit to Yucatan, Mr. Yorke once photographed a Mayan temple at Uxmal and reproduced some of the Mayan date records copied from Mayan monoliths. In the background of the bookplate, modern skyscrapers supply the contrast between the ancient and present-day civilization. The owner writes: "The sum total of human knowledge is so great; and yet we know so little. The phrase from Montaigne, *What do I know,* and the contrast between the ruins and our present-day skyscrapers is a reminder of the necessity for humility."

It was hoped that an entire chapter might be devoted to the bookplates of musicians, but these have proved most elusive of all and must be reserved for later search and discussion. Of course, musical symbols are often seen in bookplates, but the plates owned by musicians proved to be a difficult goal to achieve.

.(2 3 8).

It is hoped that musicians and collectors themselves will contribute to the amplification of the next volume.

James Webb has made three musical bookplates. In the design for L. E. Behymer, the bee forms the canting device indicative of his name as well as his unceasing activities for cultural expression in the Southland.

The design for George Garde de Sylva shows his Malibu home, a rhymers' lexicon, and a sheet of music with the well-known title, *When Day Is Done,* in evidence. An historic note is introduced by the vignette of what is thought to be the first brick house in Los Angeles, built in 1853 by Dr. William A. Hammel, who was the great-grandfather of the owner of this bookplate. The design for Hazel Runge Kimball indicates her vocal and instrumental interests, as well as two histrionic pets.

The silvery pool in Charles Wakefield Cadman's plate has enraptured a listening Indian. It was designed by Margaret Postgate and is a delightful inspiration as we recall the eternal beauty of the owner's musical compositions. Ruth Thomson Saunders' design for Letha

Lewis Storrow's bookplate is a wood engraving of sylvan beauty. An interesting combination of the musical and literary is achieved in the bookplate by Paul Landacre which Nettie Rothman uses to mark her extensive collection of musical literature. Mr. Landacre endows the abstract with qualities of special significance, whether it be for the owner or the spectator.

There are several plates with musical associations, which for various reasons have been assigned to other chapters. The plate of Richard Montgomery Tobin, shown in the San Francisco chapter, is an exquisite musical ex libris. Noel Sullivan also has a plate for volumes on musical subjects, the design by William Wilke incorporating a Wagnerian theme. The same artist has designed the bookplate of Yehudi Menuhin, which has been described earlier because of its historical significance.

Inclusion of the plates of Paderewski, Schumann-

Heink, or John McCormack might convict the writer of stuffing the ballot box, for California is the vacation land of the musically great. Whether by residence, concerts, occasional cinema contracts, or visits, these glamorous people have added to California's artistic glory by appearances in the Greek Theater, the Hollywood Bowl, the civic symphony, or the operatic stage. Perhaps another volume may yet be adequately devoted to the bookplates of the moderns upon whom have fallen the mantles of Lotta Crabtree, Lola Móntez, and John McCullough.

Chapter XVI

BOOKPLATES OF STANFORD UNIVERSITY

"The Golden Age of California begins when its gold is used for purposes like this. From such deeds must rise the new California of the coming century, no longer the California of the gold seeker and the adventurer, but the abode of high-minded men and women, training in the wisdom of the ages, and imbued with the love of nature, the love of man, and the love of God. And bright indeed will be the future of our state if, in the usefulness of the university, every hope and prayer of the founders shall be realized."   —David Starr Jordan. *

T HE various chapters which comprise the annals of Stanford University might describe, if they were to be related at length, a veritable chronicle in the saga of California, so interwoven is its background with the foundations of the state. It tempts the writer to sketch in full the thrilling story of the foundations of a modern empire, the building of the first transcontinental railroad in 1869, as well as the part played by the originators of this huge enterprise, the Big Four: Mark Hopkins, Charles Crocker, Collis P. Huntington, and Leland Stanford.

Each of these men of humble origin wrote his name in

imperishable achievement, but mention here must be confined to one, Senator Leland Stanford, who in the year 1885 made public his plans for establishing a university of higher learning in the state of which he had been at one time the highest executive. A great sorrow

had caused this plan, for his only son Leland had died in Florence the previous year. For this son the memorial was begun, the words, "the children of California shall be my children," thus becoming more than the cry of an anguished father.

.(2 4 3).

The Palo Alto Farm, located in the beautiful Santa Clara Valley about thirty miles south of San Francisco, was chosen for the foundation site. The cornerstone was laid in 1887, and the formal opening took place in 1891, when David Starr Jordan was inaugurated as its first president.

Palo Alto, meaning *high tree,* was named for a lone weather-beaten old redwood, *Sequoia sempervirens,* which has its place in early Californian history. In 1769 Portolá's party, continuing northward on the search for Monterey, camped near the site of the present campus. They observed this tree and called it *palo alto.* It was also mentioned in 1776 by Lieutenant Colonel Juan Bautista de Anza as the tree which "rises like a tower above the surrounding trees." Originally it was one of two trees, and according to the count of the tree rings made from the fallen tree, it was estimated to be over nine hundred fifty years of age.

Quite early this tree was adopted as the symbol for the official seal of the new university, and it is now seen on the bookplates in use in the library to denote bequests and gifts from various sources, as well as purchases made from funds other than the Jewel Fund.

Subject of monographs, cause of delighted comment, and treasured acquisition of many ex libris collections, the Jewel Fund plate is thought to be one among the notable institutional bookplates of America. To evaluate it properly, as well, indeed, as the university to which it belongs, one should read David Starr Jordan's *The Days of a Man* for a history of the litigation and difficulties following the death of Senator Stanford. In President Jordan's *The Story of a Good Woman,* which gives the substance of his Founders' Day Address in 1909, is told in full the story of the Jewel Fund upon its presentation by him at the laying of the cornerstone of the library on May 15, 1906. This address of alle-

LELAND·STANFORD·JVNIOR·VNIVERSITY

gorical beauty inspired Edwin Howland Blashfield to undertake the commission which was to be a new experience for this greatest of American muralists. Quoting from the *Stanford Alumnus* for January, 1913: "To Stanford men and women, there is a deeper symbolism in

.(2 4 5).

Blashfield's simple and dignified composition than appears to others. To these others Athene, goddess of learning, panoplied in her helmet, coat of mail, and owl-escutcheoned shield, seated at a portico, with scroll and laurel at her feet, is accepting the gifts of Clio, muse of history, and in return conferring upon her the winged statue, wreath and palm in hand, emblem of victory. To us there is a deeper purport—we catch the full significance that the artist intended when he made a rope of pearls conspicuous in the casket of all her wealth that Clio offers with outstretched arms. And it was this deeper significance that touched Blashfield and persuaded him to do something that he had never done before, to accept a commission to design a bookplate.

"For it may be imagined that it was no simple matter to persuade an artist who is accustomed, as he is, to the sweep and color and varied composition possible on the walls and domes of great buildings to contract his brush stroke to the space and limits of a bookplate. But when the Jewel Fund was established, and a bookplate to symbolize its meaning was desired, it was felt that Blashfield with his classic spirit, his purity of line, and his dignity of design was the man to do it if he could.

"The conception that had formed in the minds of those who had the matter in charge was this: the story of the jewels is one that will be told as long as the university lives; it will be the theme of orators to fire their hearers with the spirit of the heroic early days; it is a chapter in the annals of Stanford that will always be fresh; the story of the noble woman who offered without reserve all the wealth that was left in her hands

.(2 4 6).

and said, 'The university can be kept alive by these till the skies clear and the money which was destined for the future shall come into the future's hands,' is part of history. And so they proposed to the artist a fitting theme, Clio, the muse of history, offering gifts to Athene. With this suggestion, also, they sent President Jordan's tribute to Mrs. Stanford with its story of the jewels.

"This narrative of the devotion of a noble woman, so fittingly written, epic in its elevation, idyllic in its simplicity, was the inspiration of the artist. With enthusiasm Blashfield seized upon the task of drawing the bookplate, and soon had finished the first sketch of his composition. In it he had added a new thought, completing the story. The winged victory in the picture is Blashfield's own idea. It says a word in the telling of the story that had never been said so clearly before. Others had told of the sacrifice and struggle; he emphasized the victory."

This incomparable bookplate is reproduced by photogravure from the artist's own charcoal sketch, as this method was agreed upon to preserve the soft gradations of his medium. Since 1910 this plate has been used to mark the books purchased from the income of the fund of which the sale of Mrs. Stanford's jewels formed the nucleus.

In Jeannette Hitchcock's *Bookplates of Stanford University Libraries,* now in preparation, readers will find a complete description of the nineteen bookplates and variants used in the Stanford Library. Among these a few are noted here for immediate identification. The Branner Geological Library plate contains a portrait of the one-time head of the department, later president of Stanford. The Hopkins Library was the gift of Timothy Hopkins, adopted son of Mark Hopkins of the Big Four. His plate commemorates the collection of two thousand books and pamphlets pertaining to railway economics in Great Britain and the United States. The Stanford Law Library bookplate for admiralty and aviation law was designed by Roma Mallet and marks the gifts of the Root Senate of Delta Theta Phi.

The *high tree* affords Stanford a notably decorative device as well as an historic symbol, and it appears on several plates other than the official seal plate: the Stanford School of Nursing plate designed by Edward M. Farmer; the Lane Medical Library plate engraved by the American Bank Note Company; the early Stanford plate designed by the artist, Bolton Coit Brown, who organized the Department of Graphic Art; and the interesting plate for the Chinese Collection, in which the Chinese characters complete a design by Frances Y. Chang. The Chinese Collection is not outstanding as to content or size, but it is one of four among libraries in the United States to undertake the cataloguing of Chinese material in the Chinese language, Harvard, Columbia, and the New York Public Library being the other three.

The Charlotte Ashley Felton Memorial Library was given by Mrs. Kate Felton Elkins, and a plate designed for her by Nelson Poole appears in the volumes donated by this benefactress. With the Elkins personal plate a regulation printed label is also used, indicating Stanford University ownership. A well-planned typographical bookplate marks the purchases made from a fund established by Helen Sutro Schwartz for the benefit of the Department of Germanic Languages in memory of her mother, Thérèse Sutro.

There is a plate designed by Bolton Coit Brown for the Barbara Jordan Library of Birds. These volumes were presented to the university by David Starr Jordan in memory of his gifted young daughter whose inherited scientific propensities impelled her to amass a creditable library and collection of valuable items.

The Jordan Library of Zoology is, according to the *Thirty-Ninth Annual Register,* * "a collection consisting largely of works on ichthyology, to a considerable extent made up of authors' separates, which have been accumulated by Chancellor Jordan and members of the Department of Zoology, bound in convenient form, indexed, and catalogued. The older authorities, including Cuvier, Lacépède, Bloch, Bleeker, and Günther, are well represented. These, supplemented by the proceedings of various societies and institutions, make a collection of great value to advanced students and investigators." For this library Bolton Coit Brown designed a bookplate with the inscription: Jordan Library of Zoology Presented by David Starr Jordan. The same plate was used for the Jordan Peace Library gift of David Starr Jordan.

The Hoover War Library plate marks the volumes and acquisitions of this library founded by the Honorable Herbert Clark Hoover, which is, according to the *Annual Report* * of 1933, "now the largest collection in the Western hemisphere, and one of three leading special libraries in the world on the World War and the results of the war." The plate was designed by Pedro Joseph de Lemos, director of the Museum and Art Gallery, who has taken for design subject the bronze statue of Isis which

.(2 4 9).

was designed by the sculptor Puttemans. This statue was presented to Mr. Hoover by the Belgian government in grateful recognition of his services on the Commission

HOOVER
WAR
LIBRARY

for Relief in Belgium. Thus the statue of Isis, goddess of growing grain, takes on an awesome dignity. A translation of the inscription carved beneath the statue on the plate is as follows: *I am that which has been, that*

.(2 5 0).

which is, and that which will be, and no mortal has yet raised the veil that covers me.

In terminating the discussion of the bookplates of Stanford University, the reader is asked to consider once more the tribute of President Jordan to her who made the Jewel Fund a permanent reality:

"They say there is a language of precious stones, but I know that they speak in diverse tongues. Some diamonds tell strange tales, but not these diamonds. In the language of the jewels of Stanford may be read the lessons of faith, of hope, and good will. They tell how Stanford was founded in love of the things that abide."

Chapter XVII

BOOKPLATES OF THE UNIVERSITY OF CALIFORNIA

"What was this task? It was first of all to save to the world a mass of valuable human experiences which otherwise, in the hurry and scramble attending the securing of wealth, power, or place in this new field of enterprise, would have dropped out of existence. These experiences were all the more valuable from the fact that they were new; the conditions attending their origin and evolution never had existed before in the history of mankind, and never could occur again. There was here on this coast the ringing up of universal intelligence for a final display of what man can do at his best, with all the powers of the past united, and surrounded by conditions such as had never before fallen to the lot of man to enjoy."—Hubert Howe Bancroft. *

E X libris seem to have flourished in the atmosphere of the University of California, for it has owned bookplates since the beginning of the century. At the present time it owns a set of plates unequalled among educational institutions for local color and artistic values. It has long been the custom among universities to indicate bequests, memorials, and special departments of their libraries with bookplates or printed labels.

Indeed, in common with bookplates of libraries, these plates often play an important part in the historizing of the state.

The several hundred plates of Harvard University, to name one example, illustrate New England history from its beginning. Thus it is that this Western university illustrates, by anecdotes relating to accessions, donors, and acquisitions, Californian history far antedating the founding of the university.

Although the institutional design is perforce limited in subject, a glance at the array of these plates will delight the onlooker with their wealth of allusion and scholarly associations. It is the good fortune of the writer to have acquired many of the early pictorial plates in use before the official plate was adopted. J. C. Rowell, librarian emeritus and archivist of the university, admits to more than a passing fondness for the subject, and through his interest this creditable group of plates has grown to a number necessitating a separate chapter in this volume. From the library's extensive collection of general bookplates, a large group has been mounted according to Californian owners and artists.

Of the founding of the university, Robert Sibley has this to say in *The Romance of California:* "The first transcontinental railroad had not yet reached California. Andrew Johnson, Lincoln's successor, was facing impeachment proceedings in Washington; Indians were still a menace to the long wagon trains from the East; the clipper ships from Panama and from the Horn still sailed into San Francisco Bay, when the charter of the University of California was passed by legislature on March 21, 1868. . . . Tales of gold came down from the

.(2 5 3).

mountains; fortunes were being wrested from California land. The memory of Joaquín Murieta was still alive, and Tiburcio Vásquez was harassing honest men in the San Joaquín Valley. A ruthless country, hard to reach and difficult to leave, it gave its wealth to those who were willing to fight hard and to work, but it denied the weakling. While San Francisco, a gay reckless city thrown among the hills which surround the bay, was already renowned throughout the world, Oakland was a mere cluster of houses on the shores of East Bay, and Berkeley a territory yet unnamed.''

Although this is the actual background, the gold seekers did not come to a country entirely devoid of civilization. Indeed, there are but few sections of the United States which have been endowed with so much culture at its beginning. Thus perhaps it is but natural that educational growth has been its happy fortune.

The first pictorial bookplate to be used in the university is that of the Claus Spreckels Fund, designed in 1901 by Louise Keeler for the books purchased with donations from Mr. Spreckels and Mrs. Ethel Crocker; the former for books on politics, history, and economics; and latter for physiological books. The border of oak leaves is for this college on the campus of a thousand oaks. The allegorical figures on each side are those of the Call Building in San Francisco.

The second plate to be used is that of the Ernst A. Denicke Fund, the legend on Siegfried's trumpet being that of the immortal Goethe: *The spirit lives*. The Reese Library bookplate commemorates the first actual fund created for the purchase of books, that given by Michael Reese of San Francisco. In this plate Ceres in

.(2 5 4).

the person of a Spanish *señorita* represents abundance as she holds a basket of fruits of the earth and the vine, with the waiting harvest in the background.

A bookplate which contains some of the loveliest educational symbolism to appear among university plates

is the well-of-learning plate which marks books presented to the physiological fund. Although the plate is not thus officially named, the design might be interpreted allegorically as the fount of learning or the waters of life. On the Belcher plate the famous Californian bear holds a shield marking the books which Robert Belcher, a keen student of Californiana, presented to the university. As the bear rests beneath a roof of Spanish tiling from which depends a glorious cluster of grapes, "he has a very patient air, patient air." The James K. Moffitt Fund plate marks books of philosophy given by this regent.

The Marius J. Spinello bookplate, Andreini 151, was executed by the master, J. W. Spenceley. It commemorates in classic simplicity the brilliant early professor of Romance Languages, and was the gift of his friends at the University of Wisconsin.

There are two bookplates which indicate benefactions of foreign governments. The *Bibliothèque de la Science Française* plate marks the books which were sent to the San Francisco Exposition in 1915 and later presented to the university by the French government. This plate was designed by H. Guillaume and engraved by Maquet of Paris *sous les auspices des Friends of France*. The Mark John Fontana Fund was given for the purchase of volumes on Italian literature and culture. The *Cáttedra di Coltura Italiana* plate was designed by A. de Carolis for these books, which were given about 1924.

Among professors who have made bequests of books pertaining to their specialties are: Elijah Clarence Hills, professor of Philology; William Diller Matthew, professor of Geology and Palaeontology; William Dallam Armes, professor of English; H. Morse Stephens, professor of History; and W. B. Rising, professor of Chemistry.

The galleon of International House, which pushes from shore to shore, bringing Oriental visitors to Occidental countries, forms an ideal bookplate for this student house of teeming interest. The plate of Newman

Hall is replete with symbols of spiritual significance in a very successful design by R. S. Dodge. It is used in the books of this organization founded in the name of the distinguished Cardinal and Oxonian. In it is a portrait sketch of the cultured churchman who wrote *The Idea of a University.*

The names of Jane K. Sather and Phoebe A. Hearst are inseparable in discussions of gifts to this university. The Campanile which rises above the oak and eucalyptus trees of the wooded campus is an unofficial center to which all paths lead on some occasion during the day, and its chimes direct the classes or announce hours of student festivity. This tower was the gift of Jane K. Sather, who was also donor of Sather Gate in honor of Peder Sather. She was responsible for the Sather Library for which a plate was designed by George Winterburn, and for the Sather Law Library for which a plate was designed by O. Chapel Judson including the Golden Gate and other state symbols as features. The Hearst benefactions would fill many pages, beginning with those of Phoebe Hearst, whose costly architectural works and wonderful Piranesi set, as well as original mediaeval manuscripts, are in the Treasure Room. The Greek Theater, Gymnasium, and Hearst Mining Building are other magnificent donations of this historic family. There is a tiny engraved plate with the Californian poppy motif, the source of which cannot be discovered but which is used to mark donations from the personal library of Mrs. Hearst. Albert M. Bender, wise patron of the arts, has given a number of books to the university, and was the donor of the Museum of Oriental Art. His plate was designed by Anne Bremer.

The plate seen most often in the university is that of the official seal designed by J. Henry Atkins, with variants to indicate different bequests. Among these are the Bernard Moses Memorial bookplate in honor of a

The Bancroft Library

No.   *Mex. MSS.*

former professor of Political Science; and the Alexander Morrison Memorial, whose gift is the basis of a valuable private library. John Fryer, a professor of Chinese Literature, is responsible for what is believed to be the second largest library of Oriental books in the world. The J. C. Cebrian bookplate marks one of the largest collections in America of Spanish literature and books relating to Spain. The University of California at Los Angeles uses the official plate indicating by name panel the various memorial bequests and benefactions of patrons of learning in Southern California.

Last in the series of plates owned by the University of California are two plates which mark the books comprising the remarkable Bancoft Library. A glance at the script-lettered early plate or the modern version bespeaks a tale fraught with idealism and adventure of a high order, as these printed scraps designate books which are at once a monument to the industry of one man, as well as a literary treasure of incalculable value.

.(2 5 8).

Although the two plates needed to complete this narrative have but the terse legend, *Bancroft Library,* it is the tale of these migratory books and their owners which has made this collection the unique institution

it is. Therefore, mention must be made of plates found in the volumes acquired by the library as well as by those who have administered to its maintenance in later years. No more eloquent tale has ever been told by a bookplate, nor has its utility been so quietly but insistently demonstrated, for as the student turns the pages of old volumes in his search for authentic material relating to the California of his labors, his eye rests upon a tiny typographical, a formidable armorial, or an artistic device, to which are attached names from other lands. Intent upon his search, he passes them over, but they recur again and again until the story must be told of how they came to rest in this Western world.

Perhaps the most difficult to condense in a brief space are the remarks referring to the Bancroft Library. However, if but a single reader may refer to *Literary Industries,* the thirty-ninth volume of Bancroft's *Works,* the attempt will not have been in vain. The books which are the nucleus of this library were gathered over a period of years by the purchase of large collections *en bloc,* as well as by the most assiduous search for manuscripts, books, newspapers, or any material relating to the history of the Pacific slope down through the Central American countries. A staff of assistants was employed to carry on this work, and the private fortune of this publisher and philanthropist was expended upon these labors from 1860 till 1891.

The young Bancroft came from Buffalo in 1852, with a consignment of books from a publishing firm in that city, to establish himself in the pioneer city of San Francisco, then at the height of the activity caused by the discovery of gold. As is sometimes the case, the visitor from afar possesses the vision denied those at home; and thus it was that this man noticed the demand for pamphlets, maps, books, and material relating to the newly made state.

From a beginning of about fifty volumes in 1859 grew

the enormous library which Bancroft later collected personally and through agents in all parts of the world. In 1890 he wrote that he believed the library had more volumes relating to the sources and history of California than had any similar collection elsewhere, for the world's largest libraries are of vast numbers but of scattered subjects. That this fact is admitted today proves his industry, for the student needs only to name his subject, and the material is available on origins, sources, maps, histories, and original manuscripts of Spain, Europe, and Mexico, as well as priceless family archives from early Californian families such as the Alvarados, Vallejos, Larkins, and Hayes. After Bancroft had been collecting for several years, he reasoned: "Now my task is done. I have rifled America of its treasures; Europe have I ransacked. After my success in Spain, Asia and Africa may as well be passed by. . . Here will I rest." Then he came upon a catalogue from a London bookseller announcing the sale of the library of Don José María Andrade, seven thousand volumes direct from Mexico offered for sale at Leipzig. A large portion of this library was purchased, and today in the books thus acquired may be seen the tiny bookplate marking the books collected by a bibliophile in a country which had begun printing books in the New World a hundred years earlier than had Massachusetts.

José María Andrade was a *litterateur,* bibliophile, publisher, and publicist, who clung to his treasures with a fanatic tenacity, nor would he part with them

.(2 6 1).

except for a cause involving honor and distinction. Such a cause was supplied by the unfortunate Maximilian, whose earnest desires were entirely undeserving of his fate and who strove like a benevolent monarch to improve the conditions of his people as well as to advance the country of his adoption by all known means. When he decided upon the laudable plan of establishing a magnificent library, of course Señor Andrade was the only one

able to advise him as well as to supply the volumes to form the basis of the *Biblioteca Imperial de Méjico*. Andrade's *beau geste* was made, and the scholar was rewarded, for his collection was to remain in Mexico. Alas for history and its distressing evils! The monarch lost his throne, and the bibliophile his money. After Maximilian's tragic execution at Querétaro, but before the mob fury had reached Mexico City, Señor Andrade packed his books into two hundred cases, placed them on the backs of mules, led the caravan to Vera Cruz, and sailed for Europe. And these books were the subject of the catalogue item which at length led to their acquisition by a library in their sister republic.

The Andrade label is of the simplest pictorial design which, together with the typographical label, was in great vogue in Mexico in the nineteenth century. These labels were made in blocks of four and cut apart for later use. The design shows a clump of strawberry plants in blossom, with the motto: *Among the leaves there is fruit.* The magnificent plate of Maximilian, Grand Duke of Austria and for a brief episode Emperor of Mexico, is a simple heraldic design composed of the Mexican eagle holding in his beak the serpent of the Aztec legend. Gryphons complete the design, together with a scarcely discernible motto, *Cuidad en la justicia,* over the interlacing *M*'s of the Emperor's cipher. As the late Frederick Starr, ex librist and historian, observed:

"Few bookplates can evoke more vivid memories of a tragedy." *Ex Collectione Americana* is the legend on the bookplate of the Abbé Domini Brasseur de Bourbourg, eminent collector and erudite scholar, who had been a missionary at Rabinal, Guatemala, and later for a time in Mexico.

Domini BRASSEUR DE BOURBOURG.

Upon his return to Paris he met, during the International Exposition in 1867, one Alphonse Pinart, to whom he imparted his love for things Mexican and American, as well as the ethnological lore which he had learned in those lands.

Pinart's bookplate is an unusual design in which a pictorial is placed upon a heraldic shield with mantling issuing from the scroll forming the owner's name. The motto is: *Sol oriens discutit umbras.* Pinart was in the employ of the Russian government, investigating the material on the settlement of the Bering Sea area and the later establishment of the Russians at Fort Ross. For a time he devoted his studies to the Northwest, and after the death of Brasseur de Bourbourg, acquired his friend's library. This, together with his own, was offered to the Bancroft Library for purchase, thus adding a tremendously valuable block of carefully selected material.

The acquisitions thus sketched through alien bookplates are to be revered by students delving at their ease, without effort or peril, among these treasures gathered  by scholars and men of taste to enrich the world for ages to come. As Edmond de Goncourt consigned his books to the auctioneer's orders, he said: "The pleasures which the acquiring of each one of them has given me shall be given again, in each case, to some inheritor of my taste."

Migratory no longer, these volumes of Bancroft Library which have encompassed the earth now repose in a magnificent modern edifice under the protection of a modern university, the stages in their pilgrimage clearly announced by the plates of the inheritors of tastes which we are pleased to claim.

· · · · ·

At last, *adiós* must be written. Upon a campus of surpassing beauty, another traveller ends a journey begun at one end of *El Camino Real* and extending to its last outpost. In the shadow of a New World Campanile, chapters have terminated which were begun in August, 1933, by an odd circumstance, in a dwelling upon the site of Rancho San Rafael, that portion of land which marks the first land grant to be issued in California, given by Governor Pedro Fages on October 20, 1784, to José María Verdugo.

As silvery chimes of the Campanile speed the departure of this traveller regretfully leaving a history of saints and ships and gold—a history which in some way became concerned with ex libris—the perils seem but few as the joys blend into recollections of a largesse dispensed at *misión, hacienda,* and *biblioteca.* No *caballero* on the older *camino* in the splendid idle forties could have been so hospitably invited, *Esta es su casa, amigo,* a phrase by no means a perfunctory greeting in that earlier day  and still in use at the present. To the readers who have kindly ridden alongside, may it suggest some of the gracious memories inextricably interwoven with the bookplate owners themselves—*Californios* who overtop their literary legacies as the redwood does the chaparral.

Wise it might be for us to consider the phrase of that Renaissance patron of the arts of the book, Jean Grolier, who in a period of rarely equalled cultural richness caused to be stamped in gold upon the bindings of his own volumes an ex libris conceived in magnificent generosity: *Jo. Grolierii et amicorum.* But whether the bookplates be super libros in gold, *marcas de fuego* branded by iron, tiny woodcuts, or dignified armorials, this ex libris history is terminated for the present with the wish for you, my friends, and for *Californios y sus amigos,* that you may sense in its compilation the joys experienced in its summarizing in a *today the flower of their yesterdays.*

APPENDIX

APPENDIX

EX LIBRIS SOURCES CONSULTED
ARTICLES AND PERIODICALS

Catalogues of the Bookplate Association International. † Los Angeles: 1925-1935.

Cheney, Sheldon. *Bookplates East and West,* in *House Beautiful.* † August, 1914.

Cheney, Sheldon. *Outdoor Bookplates* in *House Beautiful.* † June, 1908.

Cheney, Sheldon (editor). *The Bookplate Booklet.* † February, 1907, to December, 1911.

Cheney, Sheldon (editor). *California Bookplates.* † November, 1906.

Clute, Beulah Mitchell. *The Bookplate,* in *University of California Chronicle.* † April, 1924.

Fowler, Alfred. *The Miscellany.* Kansas City: 1915.

Garnett, Porter K. *Regarding Bookplates,* in *Overland.* † December, 1894.

Johnson, Eileen. *Bookplates,* in *San Diego Union.* † February 4, 1934.

Kelly, Geraldine. *The Bookplate's Speculative Future,* in *The Collector's Journal.* January, February, March, 1933.

Pope, A. Winthrop. *Remarks on Some Masonic Bookplates and Their Owners,* in *The New England Craftsman.* † August, September, and October, 1908.

Spencer, Edith Emerson. *Typographical Bookplates and Name Labels,* in *Southern California Printing Teachers' Year Book,* Vol. 11. † June, 1933.

Stanford Alumnus. † January, 1913.

Starr, Frederick. *Mexican Bookplates,* in *Bookplate Annual* for 1923. Kansas City: Alfred Fowler, 1923.

Starr, Frederick. *Mexican Indian Motifs in Bookplates,* in *Year Book* of the American Society of Bookplate Collectors and Designers of Washington, D. C., for 1928. Sewanee (Tenn.): University Press, 1929.

BOOKS

Allen, Charles Dexter. *American Bookplates.* New York: The Macmillan Company, 1905.

Andreini, Joseph Manuel. *J. Winfred Spenceley.* Privately printed. Cedar Rapids: Torch Press, 1914.

---

† These titles are devoted either partially or wholly to the bookplates of Californians and the designs of Californian artists.

Bookplate Annuals for 1921-1925. Kansas City: Alfred Fowler, 1921, 1922, 1923, 1924, 1925.

Carver, Clifford Nickels. *A Check List of the Bookplates of Arthur N. Macdonald.* Privately printed. Princeton: 1914.

Edwin Davis French: A Memorial. Privately printed. New York: 1908.

Fearing, Daniel Butler. *A Catalogue of an Exhibition of Angling Bookplates.* New York: De Vinne Press, 1918.

Fowler, Alfred. *Bookplates for Beginners.* Kansas City: 1922.

Hitchcock, Jeannette. *Bookplates of Stanford University Libraries.* † In preparation.

Sala, Rafael. *Marcas de Fuego de las Antiguas Bibliotecas Mexicanas.* Monografias Bibliograficas Mexicanas, núm. 2. Mexico: 1925.

Saunders, Ruth Thomson. *The Book of Artists' Own Bookplates.* † Claremont: Saunders Studio Press, 1933.

Sidney Lawton Smith. Boston: Charles E. Goodspeed Company, 1931.

Starr, Frederick. *Hunting Bookplates in Mexico.* Cedar Rapids: Torch Press, 1927.

Teixodor, Felipe. *Ex Libris y Bibliotecas de México.* Monografias Bibliograficas Mexicanas, núm. 2. Mexico: 1931.

Ward, Harry Parker. *Some American College Bookplates.* | Columbus: Champlin Press, 1915.

HISTORICAL SOURCES CONSULTED

ARTICLES AND PERIODICALS

Argonaut, historical number. San Francisco: March 16, 1934.

Gleason, Msgr. Joseph M. Article on the San Francisco College for Women, in *Monitor.* San Francisco: May 18, 1929.

Hale, Edward Everett. *The Queen of California,* in *The Atlantic Monthly.* March, 1864.

Hanna, Philip Townsend (editor). *Touring Topics.* ‡ February, 1909, to December, 1933.

Hanna, Philip Townsend (editor). *Westways.* ‡ (Formerly *Touring Topics.)* January, 1934—

---

†) These titles are devoted either partially or wholly to the bookplates of Californians and the designs of Californian artists.

‡) Carried on under the auspices of the Automobile Club of Southern California, Los Angeles.

Lummis, Charles Francis (editor). *Land of Sunshine*. June, 1894, to December, 1901.

Pacific Cable Railway Company. *The System of Wire-cable Railways as Operated in San Francisco, Los Angeles, etc.* San Francisco: 1887.

San Francisco Call-Chronicle, memorial number. April 22, 1934.

Shuman, John. *California Medicine, a Review*, in *Medical Journal and Record*. March, 1930, to January, 1931.

Stanford Alumnus. January, 1913.

BOOKS

Alexander, J. A. *The Life of George Chaffey*. New York: The Macmillan Company, 1928.

Apponyi, Flora Haines. *Libraries of California*. San Francisco: A. L. Bancroft and Company, 1878.

Bancroft, Hubert Howe. *Literary Industries*. San Francisco: The History Company, 1890.

Barr, Louise Farrow. *Presses of Northern California and Their Books (1900-1933)*. Berkeley: Book Arts Club, 1934.

Bates, J. C. *History of the Bench and Bar*. San Francisco: Bench and Bar Publishing Company, 1912.

Benavides, Alonso de. *The Memorial of Fray Alonso de Benavides*. Translated by Mrs. Edward E. Ayer. Privately printed. Chicago: R. R. Donnelley and Sons Company, 1916.

Bolton, Herbert Eugene. *An Outpost of Empire*. Berkeley: University of California Press, 1930.

Bolton, Herbert Eugene (editor). *Historical Memoirs of New California*, by Fray Francisco Palóu. Berkeley: University of California Press, 1926.

Calderon de la Barca, Frances. *Life in Mexico*. Mexico: The Aztec, 1910.

Clemens, Samuel L. (Mark Twain). *Roughing It*. New York: Harper and Brothers, 1872.

Corti, Egon Caesar. *Maximilian and Charlotte of Mexico*. New York: Alfred A. Knopf, 1928.

Cowan, Robert Ernest. *A Bibliography of the History of California and the Pacific West, 1510-1906*. San Francisco: The Book Club of California, 1914.

Cowan, Robert Ernest, and Robert Granniss Cowan. *A Bibliography of*

.(2 7 2).

the History of California, 1510-1930. San Francisco: John Henry Nash, 1933.

Eldredge, Zoeth Skinner. *The Beginnings of San Francisco from the Expedition of Anza, 1774, to the City Charter of April 15, 1850.* Privately printed. San Francisco: 1912.

Engelhardt, Charles Anthony (Father Zephyrin Engelhardt). *The Missions and Missionaries of California.* San Francisco: James H. Barry Company, 1908-1915.

Engelhardt, Charles Anthony (Father Zephyrin Engelhardt). *The San Diego Mission.* San Francisco: James H. Barry Company, 1920.

Forbes, B. C. *Men Who Are Making the West.* New York: B. C. Forbes Publishing Company, 1923.

Forbes, Harrie Rebecca Piper (Mrs. A. S. C. Forbes). *California Missions and Landmarks.* Los Angeles: Wetzel Publishing Company, 1925.

Hanna, Philip Townsend. *California Through Four Centuries.* New York: Farrar and Rinehart, 1935.

Hanna, Philip Townsend. *Libros Californianos.* Los Angeles: Primavera Press, 1931.

Harding, Bertita. *Phantom Crown.* Indianapolis: Bobbs-Merrill Company, 1934.

Harris, Henry. *California's Medical Story.* San Francisco: Grabhorn Press, 1932.

Hill, Laurance L. *El Pueblo: Los Angeles Before the Railroads.* § Los Angeles: 1928.

Hill, Laurance L. *La Reina: Los Angeles in Three Centuries.* § Los Angeles: 1929.

Hill, Laurance L. *Santa Barbara, Tierra Adorada.* § Los Angeles: 1930.

Hill, Laurance L. *Six Collegiate Decades.* § Los Angeles: 1929.

Hittell, John Shertzer. *A History of the City of San Francisco and Incidentally of the State of California.* San Francisco: A. L. Bancroft and Company, 1878.

Houghton, Eliza P. Donner. *The Expedition of the Donner Party and Its Tragic Fate.* Chicago: A. C. McClurg and Company, 1911.

Hunt, Rockwell D., and William S. Ament. *Oxcart to Airplane.* San Francisco: Powell Publishing Company, 1929.

§) Issued under the auspices of the Security Trust and Savings Bank, Los Angeles.

Jackson, Helen Hunt. *Ramona.* Boston: Roberts Brothers, 1885.

James, George Wharton. *In and Out of the Old Missions of California.* Boston: Little, Brown and Company, 1927.

James, George Wharton. *Indian Blankets.* Chicago: A. C. McClurg and Company, 1914.

Jordan, David Starr. *The Days of a Man.* Yonkers: World Book Company, 1922.

Lockwood, Frank C. *Mission Trails.* Santa Ana: Fine Arts Press, 1935.

Lockwood, Frank C. *With Padre Kino on the Trail.* Tucson: University of Arizona, February 15, 1934.

Mighels, Ella Sterling. *Literary California.* San Francisco: John J. Newbegin, 1918.

Montalvo, García Ordóñez de. *The Fifth Book of the Most Pleasant and Delectable History of Amadis de Gaule, Containing the Fifth Part of the Most Strange, Valiant, and Worthy Acts of Esplandian, Son to Amadis de Gaule.* London: 1664.

Newmark, Harris. *Sixty Years in Southern California.* New York: Knickerbocker Press, 1926.

Palóu, Father Francisco. *Relación Historica de la Vida . . . del Venerable Padre, Fray Junípero Serra.* Mexico: 1787.

Parish, Dr. John C. Introduction to *California from Legendary Island to Statehood.* San Marino: Henry E. Huntington Library, 1933.

Phillips, Catherine Coffin. *Portsmouth Plaza, the Cradle of San Francisco.* San Francisco: John Henry Nash, 1932.

Power, Bertha Knight. *William Henry Knight, California Pioneer.* Privately printed. 1932.

Rensch, Hero Eugene, and Ethel Grace Rensch. *Historic Spots in California.* Stanford University: Stanford University Press, 1932.

Richman, Irving Berdine. *California under Spain and Mexico.* Boston: Houghton, Mifflin Company, 1911.

Smith, Sarah Bixby. *Adobe Days, Being the Truthful Narrative of the Events in the Life of a California Girl on a Sheep Ranch and in El Pueblo de Nuestra Señora de los Angeles While It Was Yet a Small and Humble Town.* Los Angeles: Primavera Press, 1931.

Sanchez, Nellie Van de Grift. *Spanish Arcadia.* San Francisco: Powell Publishing Company, 1929.

Sauer, Carl. *The Road to Cíbola*. Berkeley: University of California Press, 1932.

Saunders, Charles Francis. *Trees and Shrubs of California Gardens*. New York: Robert M. McBride and Company, 1926.

Saunders, Charles Francis. *With the Flowers and Trees in California*. New York: Robert M. McBride and Company, 1914.

Saunders, Charles Francis, and Father St. John O'Sullivan. *Capistrano Nights, Tales of a California Mission Town*. New York: Robert M. McBride and Company, 1930.

Sherman, Edwin A. *Fifty Years of Masonry*. San Francisco: George Spaulding Company, 1898.

Shuck, Oscar. *Representative and Leading Men of the Pacific*. San Francisco: Bacon and Company, 1870.

Smith, Emory Evans. *The Golden Poppy*. Palo Alto: Murdock Press, 1902.

Spalding, Phebe Estelle. *Santa Barbara*. Claremont: Saunders Studio Press, 1934.

Stuff, Harry Spencer. *The Story of the Olympic Games*. Los Angeles: Times-Mirror Company, 1931.

Thwaites, Reuben G. *The Bancroft Library, a Report*. Berkeley: 1905.

Vindel, Francisco. *Manuel Gráfico-Descriptivo del Bibliófilo Hispano-Americano (1475-1850)*. Madrid: 1930-1934.

Visscher, William Lightfoot. *A Thrilling and Truthful History of the Pony Express*. Chicago: Rand, McNally and Company, 1908.

Wagner, Henry R. *Spanish Voyages to the Northwest Coast of America*. San Francisco: California Historical Society, 1929.

Watson, Douglas S. Introduction to *The Diary of Johann August Sutter* San Francisco: Grabhorn Press, 1932.

Wells, Harry L. *California Names*. Los Angeles: Kellaway-Ide-Jones Company, 1934.

Wierzbici, Felix. *California As It Is and As It May Be*. San Francisco: Washington Bartlett, 1849.

Woon, Basil. *San Francisco and the Golden Empire*. New York: Harrison Smith and Robert Haas, 1935.

MAP

Hill, Joseph J. (compiler), and Dillon Lauritzen (painter). *A Map of Exploration in the Spanish Southwest, 1528-1793.* Supplement of *Touring Topics,* January, 1932.

INDEX OF ARTISTS AND OWNERS OF BOOKPLATES
MENTIONED IN THIS VOLUME *

---

* For further listing of artists, see Supplementary List of Artists.

.(2 8 2).

Nasi, Leonella, 45
Neste, A. van, 198
New, E. H., 110
Newman Hall of Berkeley, 256
Newmark, Maurice H., 62
Neylan, John Francis, 53; *illustrated,* 53
Niblo, Fred, 232
Niven, Barbara and Robert, 168
Noll, Maxwell Hamilton, 7, 46, 66, 113, 116, 163, 174; *illustrated,* 47
Norris, Thomas Wayne, 116, 196; *illustrated,* 196
Nugaard, Axel, 116
Nuttall, Zelia, 194; *illustrated,* 195
Nye, Margaret, 174

Oatman, Homer Clifton, 122; *illustrated,* 123
Occidental College, 210; *illustrated,* 209
Olds, William B., 36, 37, 51, 184; *illustrated,* 37
Outcalt, Irving and Adele, 88; *illustrated,* 88
Owens, Charles H., 76, 167

Pacific Philatelic Society, 21; *illustrated,* 22
Pacific Union Club, 134
Pack, Robert Wallace, 201
Palache, Myra Lumbard, 193
Pallette, Edward Marshall, 130
Palmer, Olive Holbrook, 193
Palos Verdes Public Library, 149; *illustrated,* 149
Parkin, Harry Dravo, 116
Parsons, George Frederic, 188
Pasadena Public Library, 148
Paterson, Lawrence A., 49
Patigian, Haig, 42, 212; *illustrated,* 42
Patten, Nathan van, 158

Paul, Florence, 194
Paxson, W. A., 137
Payne, Dorothy, 111, 190
Percey, Helen Gladys, 166
Percival, Olive, 104, 106, 109, 110, 147, 225, 226; *illustrated,* 109
Perkins, P. D., 72, 75; *illustrated,* 74
Perret, Ferdinand, 45
Pettingell, Frank Hervey, 166
Phelan, James Duval, 25, 198; *illustrated,* 26
Phelan, Mary Louise, 196
Phi Gamma Delta of Occidental College, 210
Phillips, Catherine Coffin, 68
Pickard, Rawson J., 125
Pierce, Annie, 88
Pinart, Alphonse, 263; *illustrated,* 264
Plank, George, 110
Plaw, Eleanor, 104
Poland, Reginald, 41
Pomona College, 208; *illustrated,* 208
Poole, Nelson, 248
Post, Harrison, 156
Postgate, Margaret, 240
Potter, Edwin C., 116, 131
Powell, Lawrence Clarke and Fay, 71
Powell, William, 230
Price, Christine, 89, 115, 155; *illustrated,* 156
Pyle, Howard, 72

Quinan, Mr., 201

Rathbone, Robert, 116, 130, 131; *illustrated,* 131
Rauschnabel, W. F., 191
Reinhardt, Aurelia Henry, 220; *illustrated,* 220
Requa, Mrs. Mark Lawrence, 181

.(2 8 4).

.(2 8 6).

SUPPLEMENTARY LIST OF ARTISTS

Because of incomplete information when the text was prepared, the names of certain artists could not be included. They are listed here, together with the names of the owners whose plates are described on the pages indicated.

Alabaster, Sidney: Dassonville plate, 115
Armer, Sidney: Goldman plate, 90
    Hellman plate, 166
Balch, Winifred Favlin: Jenney plate, 125
Carr, Geraldine Wildon: Hoose plate of University of Southern California, 206
Charles Eliot and Company: Dominican College plate, 213
Christiansen, Anne: Wickes plate, 115
Clute, Beulah Mitchell: Blanchard plate, 219
    Gerbode plate, 127
    Legge plate, 127
Crispin, Angela S.: Crispin plate, 83
Cromwell, Richard: Gombel plate, 234
Davies, Elton: Clifford plate, 166
Dickieson, Marjorie: Dawson plate, 90
Elwell, James Cady: McNair plate, 86
Goldsmith, Lillian Burkhart: Mitchell plate, 71
Goodman, John: Percey plate, 166
Marshall, Bertha: Marshall plate, 154
Oakland Engraving Company: Wagner plate, 67
Ranzon, Myrtle: Mt. Vernon Junior High School plate, 214
Saunders, Ruth Thomson: Keyrose plate, 167
    Lum plate, 128
Smethurst, T. E.: Ball plate, 220
Smith, Sarah Bixby: Jordan-Smith plate, 68
Wagner, Rob: Wagner plate, 68
Webb, James: Swisher plate, 83
Winslow, Carleton: Tafe plate, 170
Winter, Raymond: Hanna plate, 67
Wright, Katherine: Wright plate, 90